Introduction to Research

Introduction to Research

SHARON SORENSON

When ordering this book, please specify:
either **R 541P** or INTRODUCTION TO RESEARCH

AMSCO

AMSCO SCHOOL PUBLICATIONS, INC.
315 HUDSON STREET, NEW YORK, N.Y. 10013

As an English teacher and department chair in Indiana, **SHARON SORENSON** has taught the research paper to over 1,000 students. She has also taught at the University of Evansville and written eleven books for students and teachers. She is presently a full-time writer, lecturer, and in-service instructor for high school teachers.

COVER PHOTOS:
Image Bank—*Barris and Barris / Abstract of paper clips and pencils*
Comstock Stock Photography—*Cascading floppy discs*
Comstock Stock Photography—*Computer keyboard*
Westlight—*W. Cody / File folders*

ISBN 1-56765-033-3
NYC Item # 56765-033-2

Printed in the United States of America

1 2 3 4 5 6 7 8 9 10   00 99 98 97 96

CONTENTS

CHAPTER	1	2	3	4	5	6	7	8	9	10	11
CONTENTS											
Definition of research report	x										x
Purpose	x	x									x
General topic	x	x									x
Narrowed "little" topic		x									x
Audience		x									x
Form		x				x	x		x		x
Guiding question			x			x	x		x		x
Tentative plan			x	x		x	x	x	x		x
Kinds of resources				x							x
Using the library				x							
Bibliography cards					x					x	x
Note cards						x		x			x
Thesis sentence							x	x	x		x
Organizing note cards								x			x
First draft								x			
Paragraph structure								x	x		x
Introduction								x	x		x
Body								x	x		x
Conclusion								x	x		x
Revising									x		x
Transitions									x		x
Documentation				x	x	x		x	x	x	x
Manuscript form										x	x
Final draft										x	x
Proofreading										x	x
Complete model reports											x

Contents

Acknowledgments

When creating any book, a writer turns to willing friends and colleagues to serve as sounding boards, resources, and critics. When creating a very different kind of textbook, this writer turned to friends and colleagues to serve in a far more valuable way. They were test cases. They were forward thinkers. They were creativity put in action. My special appreciation goes to all of them: Dr. Norma Faust, David Johnson, Thomas Despot, Rosemary Ewing, Pat Herigan, James Gardner, Ann Seng. For their kind, gentle, and witty guidance, my gratitude goes to my Amsco editors Ed Enger and Mike Ross.

Anytime a writer devotes a year or more of her life to creativity, special thanks also must go to the family for supporting the effort. So loving gratitude goes to my husband Charlie for his support, his help, and his attentiveness.

Dear Readers,

At last, an end to the dull books about how to do a research report! Finally, you have found a book that introduces the research process in a clear, simple, easy-to-follow format.

FIRST, it's written much like a play. Meet the four main characters:

Shondra	a student in social studies class
Jarrod	a student in English class; on the soccer team
Juan	a student in science class; loves working at the computer
Ms. Kyoko	their research teacher

You'll meet briefly, or hear about, a few other characters:

Mr. Kozloski	the social studies teacher; students call him Mr.Koz
Ms. Gant	the English teacher for the three students
Mr. McKenney	the science teacher; students call him Mr. Mac
Ms. Dewey	the school librarian
Jason	Jarrod's older brother

As you hear these students and teachers talk, I think you will see yourself and your teachers. You will hear Shondra, Juan, and Jarrod ask the same questions you have. Honest questions. You will hear Ms. Kyoko give clear, simple answers. Practical answers. The four of them work through the whole research process with you. Each talks about the problems faced. And the solutions found. And always you see **Shondra's, Juan's,** and **Jarrod's** work before you have to do the same work. They will take you all the way to your finished report–even as they share their finished reports with you.

SECOND, this book takes a **cross-curricular** look at the research report. Shondra's report is for social studies class; Jarrod's for English; Juan's for science. No matter which teacher assigns your research report, you'll find what you need here.

THIRD, this book takes a new look at the traditional research report. It names and describes about **ninety forms** a research report can take. You can pick the forms that work for you, your learning style, and your class. In the final chapter, you will find **three complete models.** You will see Shondra's traditional written report, Juan's first-person narrative accompanied by a photograph and the flow chart for his hypermedia report, and Jarrod's file, brochure, map, and chart.

We've tried to make this book user-friendly. Not only can you read the material aloud like a play, you can find helpful hints throughout. For instance, each chapter includes:

time management guidelines to help you plan your work
computer hints for those of you who love technology
critical thinking hints at the moment you need them
tips and traps that students, have shared over the years
three students' progress to give students' voices to common problems
checklist summary of chapter highlights
peer editor guidelines to list ways for others to help you revise
portfolio guidelines for those of you who keep portfolios

This book is based on real students and real teachers. After teaching over 1000 students face-to-face how to do a research report, I hope to help you, too. Good luck!

Chapter 1
Finding a General Topic

You've just found out you have to do a report. Your teacher calls it a "research report."

● Maybe you have been studying the Civil War. Now your social studies teacher has assigned a research report. You must do it about someone in the Civil War. You know little or nothing about people from the Civil War. How can you do a report?

● Your science teacher wants a report on a wild animal. You are to choose the animal. You can name only a few wild animals and know too little about any one of them to do a report. How do you find information?

● Your English teacher has assigned a report. She says the topic is up to you, and you should choose "something that interests you." You are at a loss to come up with a topic. How do you find a good topic?

Every student assigned a research report has the same fears. The report seems like such a huge job. You may wonder what makes a good topic. You may not understand how to do the research. You may be confused about how to put the report together. You may have no idea how to give credit to your sources. You may not even understand what "research" means.

If you have been assigned a research report, this book is for you. In it, you will meet three students and their research teacher. Together, they talk about how to write a research report from beginning to end. You will learn how they chose their topics. How they did their research. How they put their reports together. How they credited their sources. And you will see their finished reports.

Meet the three students.

Shondra, Juan, and Jarrod all face the same problem. Listen to them talk about their reports with their research teacher, Ms. Kyoko.

SHONDRA: Boy, am I bummed out! I have to do this report for social studies class. Our teacher, Mr. Kozloski—we call him Mr. Koz—says it's supposed to be about somebody from the Civil War. Hey, I don't have one idea where to begin. Even when I figure out who to write about, then what? I'm totally lost.

JUAN: My report is for Mr. McKenney's science class. We're supposed to do ours on a wild animal. I guess there's plenty to say about an animal, but I don't know which one to do. And after I pick one, how do I find out about it? I'm like Shondra. I'm lost.

JARROD: Hey, you two don't have a problem. At least you guys have some idea what you're supposed to do. I don't have a clue—not even a topic. Our English teacher, Ms. Gant, said we should choose our own. I'm ready to give up before I begin.

MS. KYOKO: Okay, let's talk. You all sound frustrated.

JARROD: You said it! How can I possibly do this report thing? It's so much bigger than anything I've ever done before.

MS. KYOKO: Don't panic! Doing a research report may seem like a huge job—even hopeless. Really, though, it's nothing more than a series of little jobs. The little jobs are just tied to one another. If you take one little job at a time, doing a report is much easier than it seems. Keep reminding yourself:

> **A big job is nothing more than a series of little jobs.**

JUAN: Okay, great. Can we break it down? First, just **what is a research report?**

MS. KYOKO: Good question. Let's begin by defining "report." **"To report"** means **"to tell about"** or **"to describe."** Like any other report, a research report has a **purpose**. Maybe its purpose is **to tell the reasons** for saving rain forests. Or **to describe** what happened during the Battle of Bull Run. Or **to tell about** Martin Luther King's role in the Civil Rights Movement. Or **to compare** figure skaters Scott Hamilton and Brian Boitano. Its general purpose could also be to **inform** the reader about an issue or even to **persuade** the reader.

JUAN: So a research report is like any other report we've done. Except it's longer. Is that it?

MS. KYOKO: Well, Juan, there's a bit more to it than that. Most of what you've written up to now has been your own ideas. A research report is other people's ideas. You learn about them by doing research.

JARROD: So that's how it gets its name "research report"!

MS. KYOKO: Exactly! **"Research"** means **"to search again."** In other words, experts have searched out all the details on their topics. They know all the facts. Now your job is to read their words. That is, you'll search again, or re-search, what they've searched out and found. That's what we mean by re-search.

SHONDRA: So a research paper comes from what others say. It's not just our own ideas. Am I on the right track?

MS. KYOKO: You are, Shondra. You'll **read what others have said** about your topic. You'll **put their ideas in your own**

3

words. Then you'll **give credit** in your report to whoever gave you the ideas.

JARROD: I hear three steps. Read, write, and give credit. Are those the basic steps?

MS. KYOKO: Exactly! As your coach would say, Jarrod, those are the basic plays!

SHONDRA: How long does this research report have to be?

MS. KYOKO: Tricky question. No pat answer. You see, there's **no set length, shape, or form** for a research report. Your teacher may set certain limits. But the report can be only a few pages or as long as a book. It can be a written paper. But it can also be in lots of other forms or even a mix of forms. But we'll talk more about that later.

SHONDRA: Can you put all that in a nutshell, Ms. K.?

MS. KYOKO: Sure. This chart shows what a research report is—and is not:

Defining the Research Report	
A RESEARCH REPORT IS . . .	**A RESEARCH REPORT IS NOT . . .**
It is a report with a purpose, such as, to give information, to give reasons or results, to show how two things are alike or different, to convince someone to do something, or to suggest solutions to a problem.	It is **not** an exercise an using the library.

It is a summary of what others have said about your topic.	It is **not** a summary of what you already know.
It is built on facts and details from people who know about the topic.	It is **not** based on your own opinion.
It is supposed to present, in an interesting way, facts and details to your audience.	It is **not** supposed to bore your audience with dull lists of facts, statistics, and other details.
It is put in your own words except where you show you are using someone else's words.	It is **not** copied from encyclopedias or other sources.
It is different from other reports because it tells your audience where you found your information.	It is **not** done as if the ideas were all your own.
It is like other reports because it has a beginning, a middle, and end, is well planned, and has details and good connecting words.	It is **not** put together carelessly without a plan or without notes that tell where you got your facts and details.
It is any length, from five or six paragraphs to many pages, as needed to cover the topic.	It is **not** a set length, shape, or form.
It is sometimes in a variety of forms other than writing.	It is **not** a one-size-fits-all product.

SHONDRA: I think I see now what a research report is. By tomorrow, though, Mr. Koz wants us to have our **general topics.** He's already said our topic is some Civil War person. Isn't that my general topic?

MS. KYOKO: Mr. Kozloski gave you an area from which to pick a general topic. On the other hand, sometimes teachers like Jarrod's leave the choice wide open. He can go anywhere for a general topic. So Shondra and Juan, you're already one step closer to a general topic than Jarrod is.

But let me answer your question, Shondra. What do we mean by a "general" topic? General topics are far too big for a research report. That's why they're "general." Later, in your general topic, you'll find a small part that you want to do your report on. In other words, you will find a "little" topic.

SHONDRA: So when I choose a person, I will have my **little topic?**

MS. KYOKO: Not quite. Your person is your general topic. Later you will decide on a little topic—some small part of that person's life. You see, if you wrote everything about that person, you would have to write a whole book. For instance, Abraham Lincoln is a Civil War figure, and look how many books there are about him! So Abraham Lincoln is a general topic.

JUAN: I think I get it. Even when Shondra chooses a person, she still has a general topic. I have the same situation. When I choose an animal, I have a general topic. Right?

MS. KYOKO: Right. Now, Jarrod, that leaves you. Ms. Gant hasn't narrowed your choice. You can come up with your own ideas.

JARROD: That sounds good. But with no limits, I don't know where to begin. Where do I get **ideas for choosing my own general topic?**

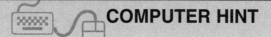

COMPUTER HINT

If you or your school subscribes to a computer bulletin board, you can tap it for ideas for general topics. One student was assigned a report on the conservation of natural resources. As a result, she was reading on a bulletin board about a college student who had chained himself to a bulldozer. Loggers were about to build a road into a state forest to begin cutting timber. That gave her an idea. She would do her report on logging in her own state's forests.

MS. KYOKO: Ideas are everywhere. Keep your eyes and ears open.

JARROD: I get the idea. Where have other students found ideas?

MS. KYOKO: They keep an active mind. They're critical thinkers. You know, Jarrod, everything—anything—you do can suggest a topic. Eating a bowl of cereal can suggest topics: nutrition, grain production, advertising. It can raise questions like why does cereal cost so much? How can cereal makers give us dollar-off coupons and still make money? How do supermarkets display cereal to get us to buy it? How does the packaging affect the environment?

JARROD: Wow, Ms. K. That's something! Who would think anything as simple as eating could help us think of topics. Is that all we have to do?

MS. KYOKO: Exactly! In fact, let me show you a summary of **idea sources.** Then we'll talk some more.

Sources for General Topics

IDEA SOURCES	GENERAL TOPICS
personal interests, conversation	scouting, electronic games, computers, church activities, camping, hiking, music, hobbies
extracurricular or school activities	sports, clubs, competitions, teams, fund raisers, school publications, school plays, musicals
family, family history	cultural background, family members' occupations, genealogy, immigrating, changes over the generations
newspapers, magazines, television, radio, local problems	endangered species, pollution, rain forests, equal rights, nursing homes, welfare, divorce, children's rights, adoption, drugs, abuse, military conflicts, political issues, nutrition, health, wetlands
school subjects	history, historical figures, science, scientists, math, mathematicians, literary figures, music, art, technology

JARROD: Well, Ms. K., that looks simple enough. But what does it all mean? How do I come up with a topic for me?

MS. KYOKO: Just put your mind in gear. Some students think about what they hear on the **daily news.** They think about **general school work.** They listen carefully to **conversations** with family, friends, and neighbors. They consider their **personal interests.** Then they **ask questions**—lots of questions—and the answers suggest general topics.

CRITICAL THINKING HINT

One good way to think critically is to wonder. Try using these beginning words:

"I wonder why..."
"I wonder how..."
"I wonder when or where..."
"I wonder who..."
"I wonder what..."

As you wonder, listen and look. Listen to what family members say. What the newspapers say. What the television newscasters say. What your neighbors say. What your religious leaders say. Look around you at health problems, social problems, environmental problems, community problems.

MS. KYOKO: Students last year kept lists of questions in their learning logs. They have let me share some of their entries with you. The first are from students who **talked with family members** about possible topics.

My dad thinks the bicycle helmet laws are just a gimmick. He says bicycle shops pushed the law to make more money.

But Mom thinks the helmets are really good. I wonder if anyone's life was ever saved by a bicycle helmet?

Grandma is always complaining about the price of bread. What's in it that costs so much?

My uncle says in Singapore a boy was publicly whipped for spray-painting graffiti. He also says Singapore is practically crime free. So should we punish crimes the way they do?

JARROD: I can hear my grandfather in that last entry. He'd say something like that.

MS. KYOKO: You get the idea. Talking to family members will help you think of possible topics. These next entries are from students who listened to **newscasts or documentaries on television and radio.** You can tell they thought about the story behind the news.

On the news I heard that the EPA can do things to a city if it exceeds EPA limits for air pollution. We have a problem with that here in the summer. So can we keep driving our cars if the city goes over the limits? What happens?

A television show talked about how some old people are ripped off by con artists. If age is a factor, then are young people ripped off, too?

The show also talked about how women on the job aren't treated the same as men. I wonder if that's true for my mother?

Working moms like mine have to worry about their kids. I wonder how many companies have child care for their workers?

SHONDRA: We talk a lot at home about the stories behind the news. Sometimes we wonder if we get the whole story. But that won't help me with a report about somebody from the Civil War.

MS. KYOKO: Maybe not. But then again, maybe so. The news may refer to historical figures. Sometimes it's just a passing reference—something that gives you an idea. Maybe a news story about a race bias case reminds you of Rosa Parks. She's one of the key figures in the Civil Rights Movement. It's the active mind that finds good ideas for research reports.

JUAN: I may even hear something on the news about an animal, right?

MS. KYOKO: Of course, Juan, or you may see something in the newspaper. Here are some learning log entries from students who watched for the **unusual or interesting newspaper or magazine item.**

> This one article told about a homeless man who saved two old people from a burning car. He seems like a good person. So how did he get to be homeless?

> This Colorado farmer says he can't take enough water from the river to irrigate his crops. So how will he grow food? The article also talked about the sandhill cranes. They can't live if the farmers take all the water. What else will die if the farmers upriver take all the water?

> Last weekend there was a big article about these people who spent months putting up over 200 bluebird boxes. Why would they do that? Can't bluebirds build nests without boxes?

JUAN: Say, here are two kids writing about birds. Birds are animals. Maybe the bluebird is a topic for me. I have to wonder, too, why those people put up boxes. Two hundred of them! Hmmm. I wonder if Mr. Mac would like a report about bluebirds?

MS. KYOKO: Now you're getting the idea! But there's more. You can also **talk to neighbors about local problems.** That may spark an idea for a topic. Here are a few more log entries from students who did just that.

> It's all the talk with the election only a few of weeks away: What will happen to our city if we have riverboat gambling? What has happened in other cities?

If the union goes on strike, how do we pay the rent and buy food? My dad says they have to strike sometimes. But what happens to families like ours?

I've heard about Neighborhood Watch groups. What can we do in our neighborhood to make us all feel safer from crime?

JARROD: These entries really show good thinking. The kids had good questions. I don't know if I'd ever come up with questions like that.

MS. KYOKO: You'll have different questions—just as good. Each of us thinks differently, depending on our backgrounds. But if you get really involved in your topic search, you'll have good results. Look. Listen. Talk. Write. Get involved. Follow suggestions. Share ideas. Think!

Put Your Whole Self into Your Topic Search

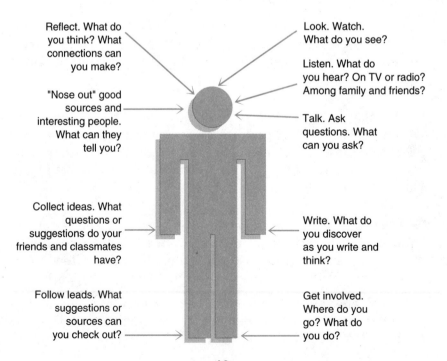

Reflect. What do you think? What connections can you make?

"Nose out" good sources and interesting people. What can they tell you?

Look. Watch. What do you see?

Listen. What do you hear? On TV or radio? Among family and friends?

Talk. Ask questions. What can you ask?

Collect ideas. What questions or suggestions do your friends and classmates have?

Write. What do you discover as you write and think?

Follow leads. What suggestions or sources can you check out?

Get involved. Where do you go? What do you do?

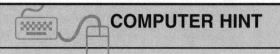

COMPUTER HINT

Use the computer for three ways to find topic ideas:

1. Some writing software includes idea generators. If yours does, use it to help you think of general topics.

2. Use the word processing program to write lists. Write as fast as you can, letting ideas flow. Print a copy. Reread your lists and let your mind add new ideas, new reactions, new connections. The exercise should help you come up with a topic.

3. Turn off your monitor (but not your computer) and freewrite as fast as you can. To freewrite means to write as you think. Don't worry about sentences or spelling or grammar. Just write ideas—words, phrases, sentences, whatever. After ten or fifteen minutes, turn on the monitor and print out your ideas.

As Shondra, Juan, and Jarrod question and think, they are exploring general topics. You do the same. When you have a general topic, you are ready for the next little job.

TIME MANAGEMENT GUIDELINES

Whether you have four weeks or ten weeks to do your research project, choose your general topic now, within twenty-four hours.

THREE STUDENTS' PROGRESS

You have already met Shondra, Juan, and Jarrod. We will follow the three of them as they work their way from choosing a topic through completing the final report. The three of them face very different kinds of assignments in different classes. So their experiences should help you meet your own assignment no matter what it is. You will hear from each of them in each chapter and follow their progress.

SHONDRA: Like everybody else in my class, I'm trying to figure out who to write about. Mr. Koz, our social studies teacher, says we can choose any person connected with the Civil War. Other than guys like General Grant and General Lee, I don't know who was interesting.

Yesterday we talked about the Underground Railroad. You know, the system people set up before the Civil War to help slaves escape? It wasn't really under ground, of course. Because the "stations" were secret, the name "underground" made sense. Well, that was interesting. So maybe I can find somebody connected with that.

I'd really like to write about somebody I can identify with—maybe a woman. But I don't know of any Civil War people like that. I'm going to talk to Mr. Koz and to my English teacher, Ms. Gant. Maybe they'll have some advice. My uncle is a Civil War buff, so he may have some suggestions, too. I'll call him tonight. I want to get on with this thing and quit wasting time worrying over a topic.

JUAN: My problem is something like Shondra's. Mr. Mac says we have to choose an animal native to this area. That narrows it down. Even so, there are dozens I could do my report on. I'd really enjoy studying any of them. But I don't want to do the same animal as someone else. Then we'd be fighting over books in the library. I've been thinking. You know, I really like photography. Especially nature stuff. So I've noticed how good some animals are at camouflage. Maybe I should do something about one of them. But which one? I made a short list. Snowshoe hare, coyote, snake, chameleon, and partridge. Tonight I'll talk to my neighbor. He's a great outdoorsman. I know he'll have suggestions. I wish my grandfather didn't live so far away. When I spend summers on the ranch with him, we watch animals a lot. Usually with a camera! And he knows all about animals. All kinds of animals. I've learned a lot from him.

JARROD: In a way I guess it's good that I get to choose my own topic. One thing's for sure. I can only blame myself if I end up with a topic I don't like. But where do I start? Ms. Gant said to choose something we're interested in. Something we'd like to know more about. Gosh, I'm interested in all kinds of things. Sports, especially soccer and winter outdoor sports. Electronic games. Reading, especially about far-away places. That's because all I can do is read about them and dream.

Ms. Gant said to think about things we've been studying or reading. That might give us some ideas. Well, we've been reading stories by Jack London. He traveled into the Yukon Territory during the Gold Rush and wrote about what happened there. We also read some poems by Robert Service, another Klondike traveler. Then for my birthday, my brother gave me a copy of James Michener's *Journey*. It's about some English guys who go to the Klondike to find gold.

You know, it really helps to talk about this. Just now while I was talking it occurred to me. The Klondike combines my interest in outdoor winter activities, reading, and travel. Wouldn't it be great to go to the Klondike sometime? Sounds mysterious.

You know, I'd like to learn more about the Klondike. I don't know if that's a good topic for a research report, though. All I know about the Klondike right now is that it's cold and people found gold there.

Boy, am I nervous about all this.

Tips and Traps

Listen to Jarrod tell about his class:

"Some of us thought we should pick topics we already know about. Ms. Gant kept saying we don't have to know anything about the general topic. That we should pick a general topic we want to learn about. She had to remind us that a research project needs research—finding out what others say.

When we finally accepted that, everyone relaxed and had lots more fun!"

As you think about a general topic, keep in mind that you will later narrow it. Just make sure you choose a topic that you like. You'll be spending hours and hours with it! Even if the general topic is assigned, you will have the opportunity to narrow it to something that really interests you.

CHECKLIST

When you choose your general topic, be able to answer "yes" to the following questions.

1. Is the general topic interesting to me?
2. Does the general topic have several parts to it that I can learn about?
3. Can I find resources in the library and/or in the community about my general topic?

EXERCISES

Exercise A: Understanding a Research Report

Directions: Review the chart on pages 4–5. On your own paper, number from 1 to 10. Read the following sentences. If a sentence is completely true, write *true* beside the number on your paper. Otherwise, write *false*.

1. A research report is no different from any other report you have done.
2. A research report must be at least ten pages long.
3. A research report always has a purpose, perhaps to inform, give reasons, or persuade.
4. A research report is, by its nature, supposed to be boring.

5. A research report is based on your own opinion.
6. A research report is a summary of what experts say about your topic.
7. A research report is written mostly in your own words.
8. A research report can take a variety of forms.
9. A research report comes from an encyclopedia.
10. An important part of a research report is crediting the sources of your ideas.

Exercise B: Finding a General Topic

Directions: Everything you do can suggest a general topic. On your own paper, number from 1 to 25. Beside each number, list at least three general topics that these items suggest. An example is done for you.

Cooperative Activity: If your teacher agrees, you may want to do this exercise in a cooperative group.

Example activity: eating cereal

General topics suggested: nutrition, advertising, use of coupons, packaging that can be disposed of without damaging the environment, grain production, competition among brands, sales displays

1. listening to the television news
2. talking to neighbors
3. listening to music
4. visiting with a senior citizen
5. doing the laundry
6. visiting another community
7. reading Ann Landers' column
8. thinking about a school subject
9. walking through a park
10. reading editorials in the newspaper
11. shopping at the mall
12. thinking about personal interests
13. studying graffiti
14. participating in an athletic competition
15. planning a vacation
16. reading the comic page
17. eating a hamburger and fries

18. watching a televised documentary
19. getting dressed for school
20. driving or riding in a car
21. attending a religious ceremony
22. hanging out with friends
23. roller-blading
24. sending a birthday card
25. feeding a pet

Exercise C: Now You Write

Directions: Respond to the following on your own paper.

1. Brainstorm with a classmate or writing group about your interests. List at least ten possible general topics for each of you.
2. Number the list of topics from 1 to 10, with number 1 being most interesting and 10 being least interesting to you.
3. Write each of the first four topics on a separate sheet of paper. Under each topic, write three questions you wonder about. Follow this example:

Wetlands

I wonder if wetlands are full of creepy crawly things?

I wonder if my community has any wetlands that are now filled in and built on?

I wonder what good wetlands really are? Why does it matter if we get rid of them?

---

4. Below the questions, list at least two ways (besides going to the library) that you can find out about the general topics.
5. Next, name someone outside your writing group you could talk to about each of these possible topics.

6. Finally, write at least one question you would like to ask this person.

PEER EDITOR GUIDELINES

A peer editor is someone in your class (that is, a peer) who reads your work and (like an editor) suggests ways to improve it. When you finish Exercise C above, ask a peer editor or someone in your writing group to read your responses. Ask him or her to respond to the following:

1. The "little" topic that sounds most interesting to me is . . . because . . .
2. Another person you might want to talk to about this topic is . . .
3. Another question you might want to ask either person is. . . .

PORTFOLIO POINTERS

You may find it helpful to keep your writing in a folder, or **portfolio.** When you finish Exercise C above, put it and your peer editor's response in your portfolio. Then, on a separate sheet of paper, answer the following questions.

1. Which general topic seems to be most interesting to me right now. Why?
2. What doubts do I have about choosing this general topic?
3. How can I settle these doubts?
4. Who else can I talk to about possible general topics?

Chapter 2

Deciding on a "Little" Topic

L ike Shondra, Juan, and Jarrod, you should have a general topic now. Maybe your teacher assigned an area from which to select a general topic the way Mr. McKenney and Mr. Kozloski did. Maybe, like Ms. Gant, your teacher left the general topic up to you. Either way, you can follow the students as they continue to learn about the research report from Ms. Kyoko.

MS. KYOKO: Well, folks, where do you stand? Have you selected a general topic?

SHONDRA: Yes! After talking to my uncle, I know who I want to write about: Harriet Tubman. She was connected with the Underground Railroad and—get this!—was an African-American woman who accomplished amazing things. This could be interesting after all! I'm ready to get going on this project now.

MS. KYOKO: That's perfect, Shondra. What about the rest of you?

JUAN: I talked to my neighbor. He suggested I write about the greatest bird in our part of the country, the red-tailed hawk. I hadn't even thought hawks, but they're fascinating! I've watched them on my grandfather's ranch when I visited there in the summer. They're like silent bombers! So strong. So quiet. What sight!

MS. KYOKO: Sounds good, Juan. That leaves you, Jarrod.

JARROD: I think I want to do something on the Klondike, but I don't know if that will work. I'm still worried.

MS. KYOKO: Well, all of you are on the right track. Let's assume, Jarrod, for the time being, that the Klondike is a suitable subject. Soon we'll know for sure.

Since you all have a general topic, let's get down to business. You have three little jobs now. First, you need to **read a little about your general topic.** Then decide how to **narrow the general topic.** And finally, **choose the audience and purpose** of your paper.

JUAN: Sounds confusing. What do you mean by **"read a little"** about my general topic?

MS. KYOKO: Go to the library and find an **encyclopedia article** about your general topic. Read it carefully. Then make a list of the "little" topics the article suggests.

[*Later.*]

JARROD: Okay. Here's part of an encyclopedia article about the Klondike. Show me what you mean by "little" topics.

Passage

Attention was drawn to the Klondike in August 1896 when George Washington Carmack and two Indian associates made a rich gold discovery while panning along Rabbit (later Bonanza) and Eldorado creeks, feeders of the

Klondike that drain the flanks of King Solomon Dome, the probable source of the gold.

The strike received wide publicity in 1897 when prospectors and their gold reached Seattle, Wash., and Portland, Oreg., touching off the greatest gold rush of all. Almost half the estimated 100,000 persons who set out in 1898 reached the Klondike, most after arduous journeys over the mountain passes in the south.

—from *Encyclopedia Americana,*
1993 International Edition, Volume 16

COMPUTER HINT

Many encyclopedias are available on CD-ROM. If you have access to encyclopedias in this form, be aware that a search may turn up dozens of entries. For instance, when Jarrod asked for "Klondike" in one CD-ROM encyclopedia, he found 24 items, some with as many as 600 references! That means the word "Klondike" appeared over 600 times somewhere in the encyclopedia. The problem was, of course, that his request for "Klondike" sent him to entries about the Klondike River, the History of Canada, the Yukon Territory, Dawson City, Bonanza Creek, Skagway, Robert Service (the Klondike poet), etc.

If you have a similar experience, choose a more specific word or phrase. Jarrod changed his search word to "gold rush" and was then able to choose only articles about the Klondike gold rush.

MS. KYOKO: From these two paragraphs, you can spot six or eight "little" topics. For instance, the first one I see is George

Washington Carmack. I have to wonder who he was and how he made such a rich gold discovery. Now, Jarrod, what little topics do you see?

JARROD: Hmmm. Well, there's a reference to Indian associates but no specifics about who they were. I could find out more about that, I guess.

MS. KYOKO: Good. That's another "little" topic. Now make a list of the rest of "little" topics you find.

JARROD: Okay. Here goes.

George Washington Carmack
Indian associates
geography of Bonanza and Eldorado creeks, Klondike River
panning for gold
geology around King Solomon Dome
kinds of publicity
arrival of prospectors in Seattle
impact on Seattle and Portland
journeys into Klondike

How does that look?

MS. KYOKO: Great! You're on the right track! You have nine possible "little" topics now!

JARROD: So a general topic is like a pizza and a "little" topic is like the mushrooms. Is that it?

MS. KYOKO: Exactly!

JUAN: That looks easy. But what if we can't find an encyclopedia article on our general topic?

MS. KYOKO: If you can't find a good encyclopedia article, go to the library and get a **book** about your general topic. Look in the **index.** There you'll find a list of "little" topics that might work for your report. Jarrod, you already have a book there. Let me see it. Now where are my glasses? I'm always losing them. Ah, here. Okay. Look at the list of topics in the index. Any of these could be good "little" topics about the Klondike:

Amusements
Dawson City
Dyea
Edmonton
Gold
   discoveries
   placer mines
Justice
London, Jack
MacKenzie River
North West Mounted Police
Seattle
Service, Robert
Skookum, Jim
Smith, Jefferson Randall "Soapy"
Supplies
Trails
   all-American routes
   all-water routes
   Ashcroft Trail
   Chilkoot Pass
   Edmonton Trails
   Upper Yukon River
   White Pass

JARROD: This is great help. Thanks!

MS. KYOKO: As you read encyclopedia articles or check book indexes, make your own list of "little" topics. Then let's talk some more.

[*Later.*]

JUAN: Well, Ms. K., we've all read and have a list of "little" topics. Now what?

MS. KYOKO: Choose one of the "little" topics for your research report. That will be your **narrowed topic**—the topic for your research report.

JARROD: Great! From the article I read, I'd like to learn about the trails into the Klondike. That sounds really interesting. Would that make a good research report topic?

MS. KYOKO: Indeed, it would!

SHONDRA: Harriet Tubman's big role was in the Underground Railroad. I guess that's what I'll do. Seems like there's lots of information about that.

CRITICAL THINKING HINT

Shondra's narrowed topic is a good one, but don't be misled by her last statement. If there's lots of information, you may be in for more work than you want to do.

For instance, many students tackle a subject that is too big for a research report. They think if they choose a big topic, they will have an easier time finding materials. True, they will find a great deal of information. But then they have a very hard time going through all of it, choosing what to use, and creating a suitable report.

Keep in mind that if you can find an encyclopedia article on your topic, it's probably too big. A "little" topic, one suitable for a research report, should be only a small part of the article.

JUAN: I know what you said earlier. The animal I choose is only my general topic. But I don't know how to make "red-tailed hawk" into a little topic. Isn't that narrowed enough?

MS. KYOKO: For the time being, yes. But you won't be able to report everything there is to know about the hawk in a single paper. After you've done more research, you'll finally choose an angle, or a special way to talk about the hawk.

SHONDRA: I think we're ready. What's next?

MS. KYOKO: The next step is to think about the **purpose** of your report.

JARROD: Isn't that obvious? The purpose is to do a research report on my topic, isn't it?

MS. KYOKO: Well, yes and no. Yes, you have an assignment to do a research report. But that isn't the purpose of the report.

SHONDRA: Why is purpose important?

MS. KYOKO: No matter what you write, your **purpose and audience** govern what you say and how you say it. Even if you are writing a single paragraph, your purpose and audience rule what you write.

JARROD: Can you explain that? I don't think I followed you. I'm getting nervous about this Klondike thing if audience and purpose are so important.

MS. KYOKO: Well, Jarrod, you like sports and play on the soccer team. Let me give you some examples from that. If your purpose is to share good news about your school's winning the soccer championship, you'll say one thing. On the other hand, if your purpose is to convince your audience to give money to buy new uniforms for the soccer team, you'll say something different. Your purpose may even be to tell your audience about the history of soccer or how it's played.

   In the same way, the purpose of your report guides what you do about many things: what ideas you use and how you arrange them; the report's length and form; your sentences and word choice; what visuals you use; how you begin and end it.

YOUR PURPOSE GUIDES YOUR REPORT

Your purpose determines...

—what main ideas you include

—what details you use

—how you arrange the ideas

—how you connect the ideas

—how long you make the report

—what form you give it

—how you write the sentences

—what words you use

—how you begin the report

—how you end it

SHONDRA: I see that purpose is important. So how do I know what my purpose is?

MS. KYOKO: Think about what you want to do in your report. Do you want to **explain** something? **Compare** two things, two ideas, or two people? **Persuade**? **Solve a problem**? For example, Juan, your report on hawks may just tell about hawks. But it could also compare one kind of hawk with another. Or it could persuade your audience to protect hawks. Or suggest a way to give hawks suitable nesting sites. You have to decide what you want to do.

What Will Your Report Do?

Give information?
Example: Tell what rain forests are.

Explain reasons for something or the results of something?
Example: Explain what happens when rain forests are destroyed.

Show how two things are similar or how they're different?
Example: Show how a rain forest differs from a north woods.

Persuade someone to do something?
Example: Persuade people to donate money to save rain forests.

Suggest solutions to a problem?
Example: Suggest ways for natives to live without destroying the rain forests.

SHONDRA: I'm still a little confused. Didn't Mr. Koz give us our purpose? We're supposed to tell about someone in the Civil War.

MS. KYOKO: Good question. True, Mr. Kozloski assigned your general topic. But you have to decide on your own purpose. Your purpose has to do with Harriet Tubman.

JARROD: You also said something about **"audience."** What does that have to do with a research report?

MS. KYOKO: Your audience is your reader or listener. And that's more than just your teacher! To avoid problems later, name your purpose and audience now. Here's why. Let's say, Jarrod, your purpose is to tell about the Klondike Gold Rush. Look what happens as the audience changes:

How Audience Changes a Report on the Klondike Gold Rush

IF YOUR AUDIENCE IS . . .	THEN YOUR REPORT WILL NEED . . .
fellow students	details about how each Gold Rusher hauled 2000 pounds of food and gear over mountains and water to try to get rich
second-grade students	a very short story of one gold miner's life told in simple words
professional gold miners	details about equipment used and methods of finding and mining gold in 1898
people who run a business	facts about business successes and failures of gold miners in and around Dawson City from 1898 to 1905
a tourist planning a visit to the Klondike	details that tell about the journey of Gold Rushers from Seattle, Washington, over the Chilkoot Trail to the Yukon Territory's Bonanza Creek

JARROD: So purpose and audience will tell me what I need to write about.

MS. KYOKO: That's right! And that affects everything you do from now on.

JUAN: Earlier you said a report is not a one-size-fits-all product. Does that mean I have more choices to make?

MS. KYOKO: When you think about the **form** your research report can take, remember this:

> **You can give information any way you can get it.**

JUAN: Just what does that mean?

MS. KYOKO: You can get information from essays. So you can give it through essays. You can get information from magazine articles, newspapers, videos, the computer, or audio tapes. You can give it the same way. Enjoy the freedom these forms give you. They offer ways to make your topic work for your audience. Just remember to look for a form that will be best for your topic, purpose, and audience. You and your teacher should decide together.

SHONDRA: You mean I could write my research report as a newspaper article?

MS. KYOKO: If that form is best for the purpose of your Harriet Tubman paper, yes.

JUAN: And I could do a video?

MS. KYOKO: Well, let's look at some of the most frequently used formats. Then you can decide for yourself.

Paper

What it is: The most common kind of report is written as a **multi-paragraph paper.** The paper has an introduction, body, and conclusion. It may include **graphs, charts, maps** or **illustrations.**

What it does: A paper can be written in dozens of ways. For this reason, it lets you meet almost any purpose for any audience. Papers can include other forms. For instance, a paper on how the endangered bald eagle has made a comeback included a graph to show the increase in population in the last ten years. A map showed where eagles are now found.

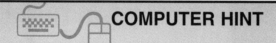

COMPUTER HINT

Your word processing software may include page layout functions. If so, your paper can take the form of a **magazine** or **newspaper article** and include **graphics** and/or **clip art.** These can be developed on the computer or scanned into the text.

Interview

What it is: A report that uses an **interview** can have **audio or video tape.** It can also simply be written in **script** form.

What it does: This form lets your audience hear the people you talk with. Combined with **role playing** (see page 32), the "interview" can be with someone from centuries ago! One student "interviewed" King Tut as part of her report on Egyptian pyramids.

Role Playing

What it is: By **role playing** you (and perhaps one or more of your peers, with or without costumes) can pretend to be a character (or characters) who is key to your report. You can role play in a **skit**. You can role play by writing in a **journal** or **diary**. You can also write a series of **anecdotes** (or little stories) as they would have been written by the person whom your topic is about. A combination of these media works well, too. Be sure to get your teacher's advice.

What it does: One girl gave a report about the mathematician Euclid, role playing as his daughter. She told the class about "her daddy" and why she was so proud of him. You can role play a similar **monologue,** or, with your peers, you can do a **news program, talk show, skit, interview,** or **debate.** These let you make a person and his or her ideas come to life for your audience.

Hypermedia

What it is: By using **hypermedia computer programs** like HyperCard, HyperStudio, HyperText, LinkWay, Story Board, and others, you can give your audience a computer tour of your subject.

What it does: This form lets you create a computer program that can include audio, video, text, graphics, and film clips. A hypermedia program uses "buttons" that your reader clicks on to access the details. One student's hypermedia program on the architecture of his state capitol building had three parts: pictures and news articles he scanned in; a biography of the architect; and his own voice as narrator.

Video Production

What it is: Everything you see on television is yours for the effort. All kinds of programs—**documentary, news, travelogue, talk show, drama, quiz show,** and **mystery**—are possible formats for your report.

What it does: Video lets you show ideas that are hard to tell about. If a picture is worth a thousand words, your video can speak volumes. A video about the local animal shelter showed the audience real dogs and cats that were up for adoption. It was a tear-jerker!

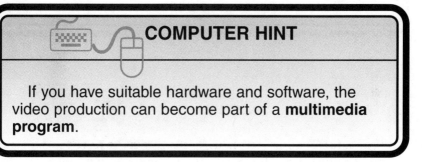

COMPUTER HINT

If you have suitable hardware and software, the video production can become part of a **multimedia program**.

Audio Tape

What it is: Sometimes an **audio tape** of sounds—voices, sound effects, music, background noise—is an important part of your report. You could also combine role playing, interview, and sound effects, and the audio tape becomes a **radio show.**

What it does: How else, for instance, could a student researcher share with his audience his report on how to identify birds by their songs?

Newspaper

What it is: The **newspaper** with all its parts—**front page, editorial page** (including **letters to the editor**), **sports, entertainment, comics, advertisements, classified ads**—can show the results of broad research.

What it does: For example, five students formed a cooperative group. Together they produced a newspaper for one day during the Middle Ages. They did a paste-up to represent the total newspaper.

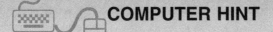

COMPUTER HINT

If you have page layout capabilities on your computer, the entire newspaper can be done at the keyboard. A scanner will let you add **photographs** and other **illustrations** or **graphics.**

Letter File (business or personal)

What it is: A collection of either **business** or **personal letters,** or a combination, that work together to send a message.

What it does: A series of letters can tell about an event from several points of view. Dated letters can show the order in which things happened. They may even show the bond between two letter writers. The letter file gave one student a way to compare Richard Nixon and George Washington. He created letters that the presidents "wrote" to one another comparing presidential problems across the centuries. Combined with other media, a **letter file** can shed new light on a subject.

Brochure

What it is: Some reports can be summarized in an **informational brochure.** It is similar to what you get in the mail advertising a product or service.

What it does: It may include **art, collages, cartoons, photography,** or **maps.** Most important, however, is the carefully written text that "sells" an idea to the reader. The text may include, among other forms, **fact sheets, case studies,** or **informational paragraphs.** For one student, it was a great way to explain the harmful side effects of using tanning parlors.

Advertising Campaign

What it is: **Advertising** appears on radio, television, and in print (as in **magazines, newspapers, fliers,** and **posters**). A **campaign** covers all avenues.

What it does: Advertising campaigns persuade. To share her research, one student used this report form to persuade her community to save local wetlands.

Résumé

What it is: A person's school, work, and professional experiences are listed in a **résumé.**

What it does: Because it summarizes, the résumé worked well for a research report about astronaut Neil Armstrong.

Drama, Skit, or Musical

What it is: Done on stage in front of an audience, a **drama, skit,** or **musical** lets a plot unfold before the audience. If the stage is not practical, a **slide show with script** may substitute.

What it does: With sets, script, and staging (and, in musicals, **songs** and **musical scores**), a drama lets the audience see and hear some event. One social studies class wrote and produced a musical to tell the story of Benjamin Franklin's contributions.

Puppet Show

What it is: When the audience is young and space is limited, a **puppet show** can do what a drama, skit, or musical does.

What it does: Since puppets are not "real" people, they can sometimes be used to communicate a great deal of information and be funny at the same time. One student wrote the script for and put on a puppet show to share his research on local labor unions.

Children's Book

What it is: **Children's books** generally have short, clear sentences, simple descriptions, and bright visuals.

What it does: Children need ideas explained in a clear, simple way with a lot of pictures. Thus, it's a good form to use for making complex ideas clear. A book titled *Plastic Man* uses pictures and charts to tell (and show!) what happens when you buy with a credit card.

Portfolio

What it is: A **portfolio** is a collection of writings like **letters, diaries,** and **journal entries**—all created by you but showing different points of view. It could also include **dictionaries, lexicons, memos, telegrams, commentaries, responses** and **rebuttals,** even **poetry.**

What it does: The collection lets you show different points of view. One portfolio tells about Orville and Wilbur Wright. It includes letters about their plans for an airplane and journal entries for just before and after their first flight.

Museum/Science/Technology Exhibit (or detailed plan for exhibit with illustrations)

What it is: An **exhibit** lets the viewer see and read about something too complex to tell about only in print. A detailed plan could be presented in the form of a **technical report.**

What it does: An exhibit uses pictures, graphs, working models, and text. It shows how something comes to be. It shows major parts and how they work. One student chose an exhibit form for her science research report. It shows and tells how AIDS affects the body's immune system.

Trial (or, less formally, a Debate)

What it is: Presented either as a **dramatization** or an **outline,** a **trial** examines all the arguments and evidence.

What it does: By using a trial, you can show the many sides of an issue and let the jury—your audience—decide. One research report on riverboat gambling took the form of a trial. The student could have used a debate just as well.

SHONDRA: These sound like lots of fun—more interesting that a regular paper. With all these choices, though, how do I decide which form makes sense for my paper?

MS. KYOKO: Ask yourself questions about your topic. The following are only a few examples.

CRITICAL THINKING HINT

Ask yourself the following questions as you think about form:

Is my topic controversial?
If so, I need a form that lets me point out different views. I can best use
— a paper
— a series of interviews
— a trial
— a debate
— some kind of role playing
— an advertising campaign
— a combination of some of these

Does my topic need visuals in order for my readers to understand?
If so, I need a form that includes visuals. That includes
— a paper with charts or illustrations
— a multimedia approach

— a hypermedia approach
— some kind of video production
— a drama
— an exhibit

Is my topic biographical?
If so, I need a way to make the subject interesting. I could use
— a paper with illustrations
— a résumé
— a portfolio
— role playing
— a scripted interview

What other requirements should my research report meet?
Your teacher may have other rules or requirements for your paper. Find out what they are.

Answers to these questions will help you decide on the best form for you.

JARROD: In the end, who decides about the form?

MS. KYOKO: You and your teacher will decide. Together you can figure out what works best for your topic, your purpose and audience, and your class. Your teacher may have specific requirements about form.

CRITICAL THINKING HINT

Think about a variety of forms. For instance, combining letters, photographs, posters, and an audio tape may work best. You might want to combine an interview with brochures and maps. You could combine a puppet show, children's book, and clip art.

For instance, Lorenzo did his research report on local architecture. He prepared a notebook of photographs. With each photograph he included two or three paragraphs about the architect or the architectural style. Finally, he created a walking tour of the sites in his photographs. To do this, he drew a map and made an audio tape to accompany it. The tape explained what people see at each site marked on the map.

Use your imagination to combine forms.

A warning is in order. Be able to give good reasons for the format you choose. Your format should be the best match with your purpose and your audience.

TIME MANAGEMENT GUIDELINES

You have four tasks to complete in a short time:
   —Do a quick read of an article about your general topic.
   —Narrow your general topic to a specific "little" topic.
   —Decide on your purpose and audience.
   —Choose a form for your research report.

If your report is due in . . .	finish these four tasks in . . .
4 weeks	2 days
6 weeks	2 days
8 weeks	3 days
10 weeks	4 days

THREE STUDENTS' PROGRESS

Follow Shondra, Juan, and Jarrod as they talk about narrowing their subjects, identifying a purpose and audience, and choosing a form. Think about your own subject, purpose, audience, and form as you listen to them.

SHONDRA: My purpose? Well, I'm an African-American girl writing about an African-American woman. I just want to tell why Harriet Tubman is important. I guess my audience is other young women and men. What else could it be?

As for form, well, that's another problem. Since I'm writing about a person, I think I could go lots of ways with this report. I could do a monologue. That could be fun—acting like I'm Tubman. Or I could do an interview. I could be Tubman and have someone ask me questions. You know, like Phil Donahue. I'd have to have it all planned out, though. Or I could even do newspaper articles. Like an article about every time she did something exciting.

I've thought about all these forms. Instead, though, I'll probably just do a regular paper. Because I want to go to college, I really need to know how to write a formal research paper. My older brother—well, he's in college and he says I'd better learn now. Maybe it doesn't sound as exciting, but I know that's what I need to do.

JUAN: I want to go to college, too, but since everyone in Mr. Mac's class is doing the same kind of paper about an animal, I want to do something to make my paper different. You know—stand out in a crowd.

I also want to do something fun, so I've been thinking. I'd like to tell the hawk's story as if I were the hawk. I think I could get into that. Ms. Gant, my English teacher, says that's called a "first-person narrative." Whatever it's called, she says she thinks it will work. I just need to tell a general audience about red-tailed hawks. I have to assume my audience doesn't know anything about hawks. Mr. Mac says we should tell about the animal's life cycle. From birth to death. What it eats. Where it lives. How it finds a mate and raises young. What kinds of dangers it faces—like in its own environment, including humans. That kind of stuff. I think if I tell it as a story, it will be more interesting.

JARROD: As usual, I'm the one who can't figure out what to do, and it's making me nervous. I think I have a purpose. That much makes sense. I want to compare several of the trails into the Klondike. Ms. Gant says I'll probably show the differences and similarities. So I thought about a series of newspaper articles. You know, like an article about some problem on one trail and another article about something good on another trail. A television talk show or a debate could do the same thing. Maybe some guys could debate which trail is best. My brother Jason said I could do the same thing with a series of letters—one from each "traveler" who takes a trail into the gold rush country. They all sound okay. I just can't decide. Of course, if my audience is my fellow class-mates, then I have to do something they will like. Boy, I just don't know.

TIPS AND TRAPS

Be careful to choose a form that gives you the best way to accomplish your purpose. Think about what these students discovered:

Last year Collette wanted to show two sides of the gun control issue. She explained, "I really wanted to do a video. I like working with cameras and television. I found out after a lot of lost effort, though, that a letter file was what I needed. What I learned was that you have to choose the form that makes sense for your topic and your purpose and audience. I really messed up when I tried to choose a form just because it sounded like fun."

David and his partners planned a hypermedia program to show how people lived in the Middle Ages. "I love computer stuff. So that sounded like a lot more fun than doing an ordinary daily newspaper. When we got started, though, the newspaper made more sense. My partners and I could have just as much fun with it but give better coverage to a broad topic. Don't we sound like journalists now? How about that 'better coverage'? Besides, we used the page layout feature on the computer to create a really great newspaper."

Katrina did a report on photosynthesis for science class. She planned to use a brochure just because she thought it would be easier than a paper. "I was really surprised," she explained, "when I found how little space there was for text in the brochure. I ended up doing drawings to give specific details for the general ideas in the text." Does Katrina have any advice? "Yes," she replied. "Just remember that a paper lets you put in more details than a brochure. Save the brochure for a report that has only a few key points."

CHECKLIST

As you think about your narrowed topic, be able to answer "no" to these questions.

1. When I checked the encyclopedias, did I find a whole article on my "little" topic? (If yes, my topic is still too general.)
2. When I look in the library, will I find a whole book about my "little" topic? (If yes, my topic is still too general.)
3. Do I already know enough to write my report without doing any research? (If yes, my topic is not a good research topic.)

EXERCISES

Exercise A: Finding "Little" Topics

Directions: The following ten topics are general topics. On your own paper, number from 1 to 10. Beside each number, write

Deciding on a "Little" Topic

two or more possible "little" topics. Check an encyclopedia, almanac, or other reference to help you find "little" topics. An example is done for you.

Cooperative Activity: If your teacher agrees, you may work with a cooperative group to do this exercise.

Example: The Mississippi River

"Little" topics: 1994 flood damage from M. R.
                       key shipping ports on the M. R.
                       most popular modern paddlewheel
                           cruises on M. R.
                       key role of M. R. during Civil War
                       wetlands along the northern M. R.
                       destruction of M. R. delta
                       riverboat gambling on the M. R.

1. Computer Software
2. The Baseball Strike
3. Computer Network
4. Expulsion from School
5. Earthquakes
6. Single-Parent Families
7. Endangered Species
8. The Persian Gulf War
9. Famous Women
10. Martin Luther King

Exercise B: Choosing Purpose and Audience

Directions: Study the example below. Then follow these steps.

Cooperative Activity: If your teacher agrees, work in cooperative groups to complete this activity.

1. Fold an 8 1/2" × 11" paper in half lengthwise.
2. Down the left column, number from 1 to 10.
3. On the first line beside each number, write what you think are your best ten "little" topics from Exercise A.
4. In the second column, name a possible purpose and audience for each. Try for a variety of both.

Example:

"Little" topic from Exercise A:	Possible purpose and audience:
Wetlands along northern Mississippi River	To persuade residents along the river to preserve the wetlands

Exercise C: Choosing a Format

Directions: Use eight 3" × 5" note cards or cut two 8 1/2" × 11" pages into fourths. Choose eight purpose/audience items from Exercise B above. Write one at the top of each note card or small paper. Beneath it write a suggested form. On the back, explain why you think the form is a good choice for the purpose and audience. Try for a variety of forms. See the example below.

> ***Cooperative Activity:*** If your teacher agrees, work with a cooperative group to do this activity.

Example:

Possible purpose and audience:	Suggested form:
To persuade residents along the river to preserve the wetlands	Brochure that can be mailed to residents that shows what happens when wetlands disappear

Explanation:
Need something quick to read that sells the idea, like an advertisement.

Exercise D: Now You Write

Directions: Complete the following.

1. First, in a complete sentence, name your narrowed, or "little" topic.
2. Next, in another complete sentence, name your purpose and intended audience.

3. Then, in a complete sentence, name the form you think you'll use.
4. In two or three sentences, tell briefly what you will do with the form.
5. Finally, in three or four sentences, explain why this form is best suited to your needs.

PEER EDITOR GUIDELINES

When you finish Exercise D above, ask a peer or member of your writing group to read your response. Ask him or her to complete the following.

1. Three things I would like to know (or three questions I would like answered) about this "little" topic are . . .
2. The two best advantages I see to the chosen form are . . .
3. Two possible disadvantages I see to the chosen form are . . .

PORTFOLIO POINTERS

When you finish Exercise D above, put it and your peer editor's comments in your portfolio. Then, on a separate sheet of paper, answer the following questions.

1. What do I like best about my topic and purpose?
2. What bothers me most about my topic and purpose?
3. What does my audience already know about my topic?
4. How does my audience feel about my topic?
5. What do I like best about the form I've chosen?
6. What bothers me most about the form I've chosen?

Chapter 3

Making a Tentative Plan

By now, you have read an encyclopedia article about your general topic. From that, you narrowed your general topic to a "little" topic. Of course, as you read more, you might make some changes to the "little" topic. However, you are headed in the right direction.

You have also thought about purpose and audience. You have thought about form as well. These decisions, too, may change after you do more reading.

Now you are ready to make a tentative plan. Listen to Ms. Kyoko and her students as they talk about why a tentative plan is important and how to make one.

MS. KYOKO: Remember, folks, that nothing is final until the final report is turned in. Till then, you can make changes. For instance, you may have to change topics if you can't find enough information about your "little" topic. You may change your purpose after you read more. And if your purpose changes, you may also change your audience. But remember,

> ## You must have a tentative plan before you begin looking for information.

SHONDRA: Why is this tentative plan so important?

MS. KYOKO: To save you time. Let's say you start looking for information before you have a plan. You won't really know what you need. So, you'll waste time getting books and magazines that in the end won't help.

JARROD: If it's going to save me time, I'm all for this plan. What kind of plan are you talking about?

MS. KYOKO: A **tentative plan.** One that will no doubt change as you work. And we'll keep it simple—just a list.

JUAN: Sorry, Ms. K., but if it's going to change as I work, why not wait until I get the work done to make this list?

MS. KYOKO: Some people do that, but as I said earlier, you'll waste hours of time.

SHONDRA: I'm sold. Let's get on with it. Can you give me an example of the plan?

MS. KYOKO: Sure. Begin by putting your purpose into a question.

SHONDRA: Oh, like "Jeopardy"! In my case, "Who was Harriet Tubman?" Is that the idea?

MS. KYOKO: That's close. But don't you already know who Harriet Tubman was? You've already said she worked on the Underground Railroad. What else do you want to know about her?

SHONDRA: Well, let's see. I guess I'd like to know how she got to be such a good conductor on the Underground Railroad. What kind of woman she was. Why she's famous. Things like that.

MS. KYOKO: Good. Now put that in a question.

SHONDRA: Okay, let me think. How about, "What made Harriet Tubman such a great woman?"

MS. KYOKO: Exactly! Now, there's your **guiding question.** That is, it will guide you as you look for information. In the end, your paper will explain what made her a great woman. In other words,

> **Your paper will answer your guiding question.**

CRITICAL THINKING HINT

Be sure your guiding question needs more than a simple answer. If your guiding question can be answered with "yes," "no," or with only a few words, it's not a good question.

JUAN: So a plan is nothing more than a question? I thought you said something about a list.

MS. KYOKO: You begin with the question. Then you make the **list.**

SHONDRA: What goes in the list?

MS. KYOKO: The ideas you need to answer your guiding question.

JUAN: You mean we just dream up these ideas on our lists?

MS. KYOKO: Based on the little reading you've done, yes. But let me explain with some examples. Juan, what is your guiding question?

JUAN: I think it's "What is a red-tailed hawk's life like?"

MS. KYOKO: Good enough. What do you need to know in order to answer that question? Give us a list.

JUAN: Okay. Let's see. I need to know what it eats. Where it lives. How it chooses a mate. Where it nests. How it raises its young. Things like that.

MS. KYOKO: Exactly! Now put that in a list like this:

What is the red-tailed hawk's life like?
eating habits
living environment
choosing a mate
where it nests
caring for young

Can you think of anything else you might need to know?

CRITICAL THINKING HINT

When you make your list, think about your audience and what they need know. To help you think about audience, you may want to work with peers or a writer's group. Ask them to be your audience. What do they need to learn from your report to understand your subject?

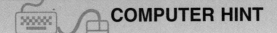

COMPUTER HINT

Some software packages include prewriting activities. They ask questions, direct your thinking, even take on the role of audience. Although many programs don't go far enough for this assignment, they do help get rid of writer's block. Some even change lists into working outlines.

JARROD: If I read Juan's paper, I'd want to learn how a red-tailed hawk hunts. Is it true that hawks kill livestock?

MS. KYOKO: Add that to your list, Juan!

JUAN: Say, my list is really growing! I can already see what my report should have in it when it's finished.

MS. KYOKO: Good, Juan, your **plan** is working out just fine.

JUAN: My plan? You mean this list is my plan?

MS. KYOKO: Bingo! Now wasn't that easy?

JUAN: Sure. But does that mean I'm stuck with this as a plan?

MS. KYOKO: Of course not. Remember, it's tentative. It can change. As you read and learn more about your topic, you may add some things. You may also take some things out. But you need to have a sense of direction before we go out looking for material—in the library or wherever.

JARROD: I think I see where I'm supposed to go with this. But I'll have to do lots more reading before I can make a plan. My list isn't as easy as yours, Juan. I don't know enough about the trails into the Klondike to write a list. Maybe my topic is too hard.

MS. KYOKO: Remember, Jarrod, you don't need to know anything more about your "little" topic yet. You're just listing the things you want to find out about. Then when you read, you'll know what's important. Think of this list as a map for a treasure hunt. It will help you find the right material.

JARROD: This whole research thing *is* a mystery. But I'm hanging in there. So far, at least.

MS. KYOKO: Great! Now let's have all of you get on with your plans. Write your guiding question. Then write a list of ideas that will help you answer the question.

Time Management Guidelines

You have two tasks to complete quickly. They require no additional reading or library work—just thinking:

—Write a guiding question, one that will later direct your reading.
—Write a tentative plan. The plan can be

● a list of ideas that you think you should talk about, and/or
● a list of questions you think your reader might want answered about your topic.

Remember, your tentative plan can also be a concept web like Jarrod's.

If your report is due in . . .	finish these two tasks in . . .
4 weeks	1 day
6 weeks	1 day
8 weeks	1 day
10 weeks	1 day

THREE STUDENTS' PROGRESS

Shondra, Juan, and Jarrod share what worked (and didn't work) for them. Maybe their experiences will help you.

SHONDRA: I think I have a decent guiding question: What makes Harriet Tubman such a great woman? I don't know the answer. But I do know that the two encyclopedia articles I read say she was quite a woman. She's in all the history books, too. That tells me something, but I'm not sure what. So I came up with a list of ideas that have something to do with "great." Here's my list, just based on the encyclopedia articles:

What makes Harriet Tubman a great woman?
    escaped slavery
    rescued parents/family/friends/neighbors
    conductor, Underground Railroad
    no education?
    preparation for military
    military life later
    clever actions
    worked with abolitionists

Some of these ideas are kind of the same. Like, her "clever actions" helped her "escape slavery." But Ms. K. said not to worry about that right now. She said just list ideas that seem to answer the guiding question. That works for me.

JUAN: I'm pretty well set. With Ms. K.'s help and Jarrod's questions, I think I have a decent guiding question and tentative plan. Here's mine:

What is a red-tailed hawk's life like?
   eating habits
   living environment
   choosing a mate
   where it nests
   caring for young
   hunting habits

JARROD: Okay. That leaves me. I can come up with a question. I think this one will work: What trails did the gold seekers take to the Klondike? But now I'm having trouble making a list. I mean, if I name maybe three main trails, what else is there to list?

JUAN: Sure, that's all you come up with if you use that question. Why not change the question a little? See, I'd like to know what problems those guys faced. I mean, it's really cold up there. How did they survive? And aren't there some really high mountains? Was there any way into the gold fields without going across the mountains?

JARROD: Oh, I see what you mean. Instead of asking, "What trails did they take?" I could ask "What problems did they face on each of the trails?"

SHONDRA: I think that's a better question, Jarrod. And I'd like to know how long it took them to get to the gold fields. What did they eat? Where did they live? And isn't it dark all the time in the winter that far north? Sounds miserable to me. Was it?

JARROD: Hey, I'm getting the idea now. And Ms. K. said to try making something she calls a web to help me come up with more ideas. Will you guys help me with a web?

JUAN: Sure. Let's do it now.

Jarrod's Web

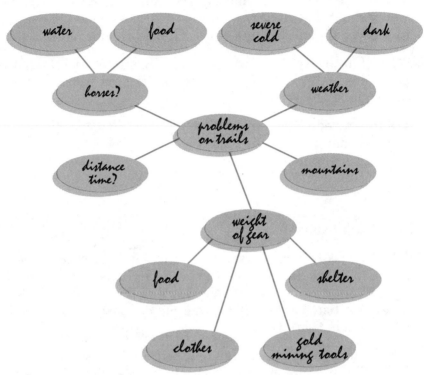

TIPS AND TRAPS

Students often face a big temptation to skip making a tentative plan. It is best to resist that temptation.

JARROD: Even though this is all really confusing to me, I've had some advice I can trust. Jason, my older brother, did his research report last year. He didn't bother with a guiding question or tentative plan. Said it wasn't worth worrying about. He just went to the library and hauled home everything he could find on his topic. Then he went nuts. You know—trying to read through all that stuff and figure out what to use and what not to use. I can see how this tentative plan will make things easier for us. And our English teacher, Ms. Gant, wants to see our plans before we get too far along. She says a plan can become an outline later.

SHONDRA: I've finally quit worrying about my list. I tried and tried to make it just right. Finally, Ms. K. said since this is a *tentative* plan, it will probably change. And it's okay to change it. Maybe often. Without a plan, though, we'd all be nowhere. I sure don't want to waste time. I can see now how the plan will keep me from doing that.

JARROD: The best tip I've heard was to think about my audience. You know, like what questions would they want answered about my subject. That meant I could turn to you guys to help me! You'll eventually be my audience, so you were great to tell me what you wanted to know. Since I can ask you, I don't have to worry so much. Kind of like soccer! The fans tell you what they like—and don't like! No question.

JUAN: It's true what Ms. K. said:

> **All of us together know more than any one of us alone.**

I'm glad we have each other to bounce ideas around. That's helped me, too.

CHECKLIST

As you write your guiding question and tentative plan, be able to answer "yes" to all of the following questions.

1. Does my guiding question need more than a simple "yes" or "no" answer?
2. Does my guiding question need more than a few words or sentences to answer it?
3. Does my tentative plan guess at my readers' questions?
4. Does my tentative plan suggest answers to my guiding question?

EXERCISES

Exercise A: Writing the Guiding Question

Directions: The following pairs of guiding questions include one weak question and one better question. Number your paper from 1 to 10. Beside the corresponding number, write the letter of the *better* question. Then, in one sentence, tell why your choice is better.

1. a. What is a landfill?
   b. How is a safe landfill built?
2. a. Was Benjamin Franklin a statesman?
   b. How does one of Benjamin Franklin's inventions affect us today?
3. a. How do geese know where and when to fly south?
   b. When do geese migrate north and south?
4. a. What effect did the Boston Tea Party have?
   b. What happened in Boston at the beginning of the American Revolution?
5. a. Did the gold recovered from the sunken *Central American* amount to a billion dollars?
   b. How did scientists recover the gold from the sunken *Central American*?
6. a. How are major exports shipped from the midwestern United States?
   b. What are the major exports from the midwestern United States?
7. a. What makes foxes a nuisance?
   b. Do foxes help or harm farmers?

8.   a. Which CD-ROM encyclopedia is the best?
      b. What makes one CD-ROM encyclopedia better than another?

9.   a. What are the common characteristics of Heisman Trophy winners?
      b. Which college team has had the most Heisman Trophy winners?

10.   a. Who was the last President to be born in a log cabin?
      b. How did James Garfield come to be a U.S. President?

Exercise B: Studying Tentative Plans

Directions: Review the tentative plans shown in this chapter by thinking about and discussing the following questions.

Cooperative Activity: If your teacher agrees, complete this activity in a cooperative group.

1. Shondra made her tentative plan (page 52) after reading only two encyclopedia articles. As a result, is it workable for a tentative plan? Why or why not?

2. Juan's tentative plan (page 53) is based on conversations with Ms. Kyoko, Jarrod, and Shondra. Do you think his tentative plan is acceptable? Why or why not?

3. Jarrod's tentative plan is in the form of a concept web (page 54). Put the web in the form of a list similar to Shondra's tentative plan.

4. Is Jarrod's tentative plan (in the form of a web or a list) acceptable? Why or why not?

5. Which of the three tentative plans do you think is the best? Why?

Exercise C: Now You Write

Directions: On your own paper, respond to the following.

1. Write your guiding question.

2. Write a tentative plan, either as a list (like Shondra's or Juan's) or as a web (like Jarrod's). Make sure the tentative plan answers your guiding question.

PEER EDITOR GUIDELINES

When you finish Exercise C, ask a peer editor or someone in your writing group to read your work. He or she should use the following guidelines to react.

1. After I read your guiding question, I am most interested in learning about . . .
2. After I read your guiding question, I wondered about . . .
3. The part of your tentative plan I like best is . . .
4. In addition to what you list on your tentative plan, you might want to add . . .

PORTFOLIO POINTERS

When you finish Exercise C and your peer editor responds to your guiding question and tentative plan, put both papers in your portfolio. Then answer these questions.

1. What do I like best about my tentative plan?
2. What questions do I still have about my tentative plan?
3. Where/how can I find the answers to these questions?

Chapter 4

Searching
the Library

Your tentative plan is in place. Now is the time to look for resources, which can be found in various forms and places.

SHONDRA: These **resources** we have to find, just what do
they include?

MS. KYOKO: Resources can be in many forms. They can be
print. That's what most of them are. Print can involve books,
newspapers, magazines, pamphlets, or even on computer or
CD-ROM.

JUAN: Computer stuff! Now you're talking my language! I
hadn't thought about computer and CD-ROM things being
part of print, but of course they are. And Mr. Mac will love
it if we use some kind of technology for our science reports.
But you said resources can be in many forms. What else?

MS. KYOKO: Resources can also be **visual.** Like videos, slides,
charts, maps, videodiscs—things like that. And resources can
also be **auditory.** Things you listen to—like cassette tapes,
speeches, sermons, concerts, or radio programs.

JARROD: Well, that really gives us lots to choose from! Ms. Gant will be happy with us if we can use all these things.

MS. KYOKO: And we're not finished! Resources can also be people. Live people. People you talk with or listen to. That's part of the list of auditory resources.

SHONDRA: What a list! I bet I can even impress Mr. Koz with all this! Can we write it down? Otherwise I'll forget what you've said.

MS. KYOKO: Sure. We can even put it all in a little chart. We'll list the three kinds of resources and some examples of each.

PRINT

books	pamphlets
magazines	brochures
microfilm	microfiche
newspapers	maps
computer data banks	CD-ROM

VISUAL

photographs	videodiscs
transparencies	fine art
filmstrips	video tapes
posters	television
slides	

AUDITORY

radio	audio tapes
public speeches	plays
musicals	concerts
sermons	interviews
compact disks	

JARROD: So all the resources are in the library?

MS. KYOKO: Many are, but you can find resources elsewhere, too. For instance, you can **interview** someone. You can do an **experiment,** or take a **survey.** Maybe you fax or write someone. Their **response** becomes a resource. Maybe you go to a **show** or **concert,** or join in an **activity.** What you learn as a result is first-hand research.

JARROD: Now I'm worried again. Do we have to use all these different resources? Can't we just go to the library, check out some books or magazines, and call it quits?

MS. KYOKO: Sure. That's what many students do. But the research is more fun if you have a chance to include other resources as well.

SHONDRA: I see what you mean. But I have a problem. It's a little hard to interview Harriet Tubman. I can't imagine I'll find any resources outside the library.

MS. KYOKO: It's true that interviews aren't always practical. But remember the uncle you talked about—the one who's a Civil War buff? He might be great to interview!

SHONDRA: Oh, I get it. And Uncle Ross really loves to talk and talk and talk about the Civil War. Maybe he does know something about Tubman. Hummm.

JUAN: Say, that gives me an idea, too. Since my subject is the red-tailed hawk, I could interview a wildlife biologist. There's a guy at the nature center who might be good to interview. He's always been nice about answering my questions when I've been there. That would be a lot more interesting that just reading about hawks.

MS. KYOKO: Good idea. After you do your basic research, you should make plans for an interview.

JUAN: Why *after* I do my basic research? Why not do the interview right away? It'll save me time.

MS. KYOKO: Probably not. You see, whoever you're interviewing may feel put upon if you come empty headed. They don't want you to take hours of their time because you're too lazy to look up the basic information. So you need to learn as much about your topic as you can first. Then get to the nitty-gritty during the interview.

JARROD: I get it! If I'm going to talk to somebody about soccer, I want them to know at least the basic plays. Then we can get into the really interesting stuff.

MS. KYOKO: Exactly! And of course, you'll need to plan your interview. Call for an appointment. Write out your questions; maybe even send your questions ahead of time. Plan your interview so you won't waste time—theirs or yours.

JUAN: You mean I can't just show up and ask questions?

SHONDRA: Only if you want to talk to Uncle Ross all night about the Civil War!

MS. KYOKO: [*Laughing.*] Well said, Shondra! Seriously, though, people have busy schedules. An interview takes away from their time. So we all have to be careful that we don't interrupt.

JUAN: Oh. I hadn't though of that. It would be pretty rude to just show up. What else have I not thought of?

MS. KYOKO: You'll want to check with your parents. And with Mr. McKenney. Just to make sure your doing an interview is okay with them. And then you'll want to be prepared to take notes, maybe even tape record the interview so you don't forget or miss something important. And you'll want to follow up with a thank-you letter.

JUAN: Sounds like an inteview is a lot more than just going to talk to somebody!

MS. KYOKO: Good observation, Juan! So what other questions do any of you have about resources?

JARROD: I'm still back here on the basic stuff. First off, I'm not great at finding things in the library, and I'm going to need all kinds of stuff. Like maps that show the Klondike trails. And dates of the Gold Rush. And details about the different trails. Where do I start?

MS. KYOKO: There are three parts to the library: **general reference, nonfiction,** and **fiction.** You probably won't be using fiction, but you need to know your way around the rest of the library.

THREE PARTS OF THE LIBRARY

general reference
nonfiction
fiction

JUAN: Let's start with general reference. What's there?

MS. KYOKO: You find everything from dictionaries to encyclopedias in **general reference.** These books are called *reference* books because you refer to them to find bits of information. People don't read reference books from cover to cover.

JARROD: So if I'm looking for dates and maps, I'll be checking out books from the reference section?

MS. KYOKO: You'll certainly use those books, but you can't check them out. Don't worry, though. Remember, you'll only need little bits and pieces from any one book—a map here, a date there. You find what you need and take notes or make photocopies. Just don't forget to make a note of the book's title, author, and publishing details. More on that later.
First, here's a list of the kinds of books you'll find in the reference section:

dictionaries—including general dictionaries, abridged and unabridged, for English and foreign languages, like

Webster's New World Dictionary, or subject-specific dictionaries that focus only on one topic, like *The International Dictionary of Thoughts* and the *Dictionary of Problem Words and Expressions*

encyclopedias—including general information sources, like *Encyclopedia Americana,* or subject-specific sources that focus only on one topic, like *Current Biography* or *Encyclopedia of Social Sciences*

indexes—references that show where information can be found, like the *New York Times Index,* the *Readers' Guide to Periodical Literature,* and *Book Review Digest*

yearbooks—annual listings of a single year, like *Facts on File* and *Statesman's Yearbook*

almanacs—storehouse of miscellaneous facts and statistics, published annually, like the *World Almanac and Book of Facts* and *Statistical Abstract of the United States*

COMPUTER HINT

Many general references are in electronic form. Your library may have encyclopedias on CD-ROM (compact disc, read only memory). You may also find on CD-ROM history books, dictionaries, and other reference books. You can make quick subject searches on CD-ROM because it lets you search in many ways with just a few keystrokes. If your library has CD-ROM, find out what references and/or indexes are on the system. Most are easy to use, so you'll need only a little coaching.

Remember, the computer can be hooked to a printer. So you can print out pages from these references. This allows you to take materials home even though general references cannot be checked out.

biographical dictionaries—collections of sketches of lives of individuals, like *Current Biography* or *Who's Who in America*

atlases—books of maps and charts, like the *American Heritage Pictorial Atlas of United States History*

periodical publications—newspapers, newsletters, and journals, like *The New York Times* and *U.S. News and World Report*

SHONDRA: So general reference will have the maps Jarrod needs. Now, how about some hints for finding other kinds of **nonfiction** books?

MS. KYOKO: Nonfiction books in most libraries are numbered and arranged by what we call the **Dewey Decimal System**. Its ten main classes are arranged like this:

DEWEY DECIMAL SYSTEM

000 - Generalities
100 - Philosophy
200 - Religion
300 - Social Sciences
400 - Languages
500 - Pure Science
600 - Technology
700 - Art and Recreation
800 - Literature
900 - History

So, if you need a book about Harriet Tubman during the Civil War, you'll find it in the 900s. The card catalog or computer catalog will tell you its exact number so you can locate it.

JARROD: What's the difference between a card catalog and a computer catalog?

MS. KYOKO: In many libraries computer catalogs have re-placed card catalogs. They work about the same way, so let's begin with the **card catalog.** Each nonfiction book has three kinds of cards: **subject card, title card,** and **author card.** You'll use mostly **subject cards.** Let's look at an example.

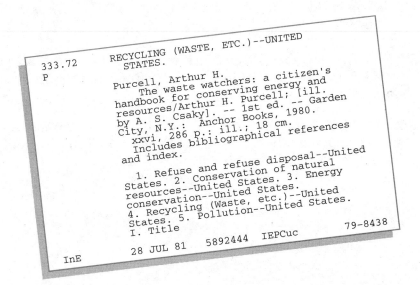

```
333.72       RECYCLING (WASTE, ETC.)--UNITED
  P            STATES.
             Purcell, Arthur H.
               The waste watchers: a citizen's
             handbook for conserving energy and
             resources/Arthur H. Purcell; [ill.
             by A. S. Csaky]. -- 1st ed. -- Garden
             City, N.Y.: Anchor Books, 1980.
               xxvi, 286 p.: ill.; 18 cm.
               Includes bibliographical references
             and index.

               1. Refuse and refuse disposal--United
             States. 2. Conservation of natural
             resources--United States. 3. Energy
             conservation--United States.
             4. Recycling (Waste, etc.)--United
             States. 5. Pollution--United States.
             I. Title                            79-8438
  InE         28 JUL 81   5892444   IEPCuc
```

JARROD: Hey, even I can see the subject. That's the first big heading. "Recycling (Waste, etc.)—United States." Then the author's name, Arthur H. Purcell. And then the book title, *The Waste Watchers: A Citizen's Handbook for Conserving Energy and Resources.* That's the important stuff. But, from there on I'm lost. What are all these other words and numbers?

MS. KYOKO: For your purposes, there are two important details. First, see the library call number in the upper left corner? It tells you where to find the book in the library.

SHONDRA: Okay. This one is 333.72 P. So that's in the Social Sciences section, right?

MS. KYOKO: Exactly. And remember, when you find 333.72 P that other books on the same topic will be shelved nearby.

CRITICAL THINKING HINT

When you find a useful book on the shelf, look at the six or eight books on either side. Since books are shelved by subject, other books on your topic will probably be nearby. Check the books by skimming the tables of contents and indexes. You may find something your catalog search missed.

JARROD: I like that idea. But you said there were two important details. What's the second?

MS. KYOKO: Okay. Look at the note line in the middle of the card that begins "Includes." It tells you whether the book has an index or other helpful features.

JUAN: Looks like this one has a bibliography and an index. So Purcell lists other books on the subject and gives an index for finding "little" topics. If my report were on recycling, these could be a real help.

JARROD: With help like this, maybe I should change my topic!

MS. KYOKO: [*Laughing.*] I don't think that will be necessary, Jarrod. After all, you'll find the same kind of help when you look up your own topic. Then the note line can help you decide whether or not to hunt for the book on the shelf.

SHONDRA: I'm with you on everything so far. But what are all the numbered items on the bottom half of the card?

MS. KYOKO: The items numbered 1-5 are other subject headings where you can find this same book listed.

SHONDRA: That seems like so much wasted print. Why would I want to know that?

MS. KYOKO: Can anybody guess?

JUAN: Well, maybe. Like if I'm looking for something about recycling, I'd know that I could also look under "Refuse and Refuse Disposal," "Conservation of Natural Resources," "Energy Conservation," and "Pollution." Wouldn't these headings have books I need?

MS. KYOKO: Probably so. And that's exactly why you want to look at the other subject headings.

SHONDRA: So this card gives us all kinds of clues about a book before we even look for it on the shelf.

MS. KYOKO: Right! Clues about this book and clues about where to find other related books. You can even tell how long the book is. This one is 286 pages. You can tell whether it's new or old. This book was published in 1980. So if you need something really up-to-date about recycling, this one is too old.

SHONDRA: Hey, that's really practical!

JUAN: The card catalog seems so simple to use, but sometimes I don't find what I need. In fact, I looked up "red-tailed hawk" and found nothing. Then I tried "hawk." Still nothing. Does that mean the library doesn't have any books on hawks?

MS. KYOKO: Maybe. But then you don't need a whole book about hawks, do you? Remember, if you find a whole book on your subject, your subject is too broad!

JUAN: Oh, that's right. I remember. But how do I find stuff about my topic?

MS. KYOKO: When you don't find your topic, try to come up with another word. You were right to look under "hawk" instead of "red-tailed." You might also try a broader subject, like "birds."

CRITICAL THINKING HINT

When you don't find your "little" subject in the catalog, try the general subject. For instance, a hawk is a kind of bird, so look under "birds." When you find the books about birds in general, look in the index to find the specific pages about hawks. Then on those pages you should find something specifically about red-tailed hawks.

CAUTION: Remember, your "little" subject should not be so big that whole books are written about it!

JARROD: You also mentioned author cards and title cards. How are they different from subject cards?

MS. KYOKO: The only real difference is the way they are alphabetized in the card catalog. Take a look at this **author card.** What looks different?

E
78
.S7
R6

Rodee, Marian E.
    Southwestern weaving/Marian E.
Rodee. 1st ed. Albuquerque: University
of New Mexico Press, c1977.
    x, 176 p.: ill. (some col.); 27 cm.
    A catalog of textiles from the
collection of the Maxwell Museum of
Anthropology, University of New Mexico.
    Bibliography: p. 175--176.

    1. Indians of North America--
Southwest, New--Textile industry and
fabrics--Catalogs. 2. Navaho Indians--
Textile industry and fabrics--Catalogs.
3. Maxwell Museum of Anthropology.
I. Maxwell Museum of Anthropology
II. Title

76-21517

InEU   28 NOV 78   3420880   IUEUuc

JARROD: The only thing I see that's different is the top line. This one gives the title on the top line while the other one gave the subject.

MS. KYOKO: Exactly.

JUAN: Well, then, if they're so much alike, why have both cards in the catalog?

MS. KYOKO: Good question. Let's say, Juan, that you find a really good book about hawks. You may want to look up the author to see if he or she has written anything else about hawks. Often a good writer will do more than one book about a subject that he or she knows well.

SHONDRA: Okay. That leaves the **title card.** Is it about the same, too?

MS. KYOKO: Yes. Look at this example. Notice that the top line is now the book title.

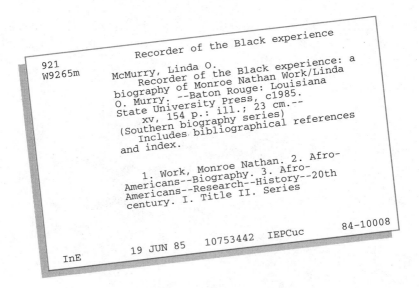

921
W9265m

Recorder of the Black experience

McMurry, Linda O.
Recorder of the Black experience: a biography of Monroe Nathan Work/Linda O. Murry. --Baton Rouge: Louisiana State University Press, c1985.
xv, 154 p.: ill.; 23 cm.--
(Southern biography series)
Includes bibliographical references and index.

1. Work, Monroe Nathan. 2. Afro-Americans--Biography. 3. Afro-Americans--Research--History--20th century. I. Title II. Series

InE   19 JUN 85   10753442   IEPCuc   84-10008

JARROD: When would we ever use title cards?

MS. KYOKO: They probably are the least used of the three kinds of cards. But let's say someone recommends a good

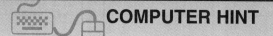

COMPUTER HINT

Each computer catalog is a little different, but there are some general patterns. The next several pages talk about the kinds of searches you can do on most computer catalogs.

book about the Klondike. She knows the title but not the author. You can find it by looking up the title card.

SHONDRA: Okay. I think we're tuned in to the card catalog. Earlier you said the card catalog and the computer catalog are similar. I take it that means there are some differences. What do we need to know about **computer catalogs?**

MS. KYOKO: The idea is similar, but generally computer catalogs are faster and easier to use. Computer catalogs have the same three searches as the card catalog: title, author, and subject. Many computer catalogs also have something called a keyword search.

JARROD: "Keyword search" sounds like the same thing as "subject search." What's the difference?

MS. KYOKO: Good question. For instance, Jarrod, your topic—or subject—is the Klondike. If you did a keyword search, you would get a list of every use of the word Klondike—Klondike River, Klondike region, Klondike gold rush, history of Canada's Klondike, poems by Robert Service about the Klondike, and so on.

JARROD: That's scary. I don't want all that stuff. So why would I ever want to do a keyword search?

JUAN: Hey, Jarr! That's the whole point! A "key" word is not the same as subject. Klondike is your subject, but a keyword

Computer Catalog

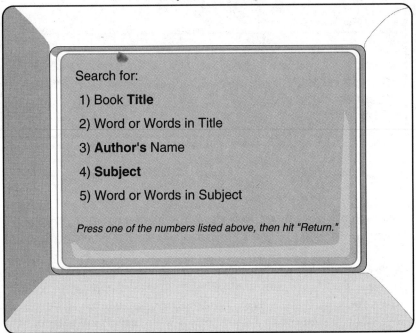

Search for:

1) Book **Title**

2) Word or Words in Title

3) **Author's** Name

4) **Subject**

5) Word or Words in Subject

Press one of the numbers listed above, then hit "Return."

may be "trail" or "Yukon" or "gold rush." Let's say you put "Klondike" and "trail" together, then most computer catalogs will list only books that have both words in them.

MS. KYOKO: That's right, Juan. You've been working on this information highway long enough to have figured out lots of little hints.

JARROD: He's into computers the way I'm into soccer. This information highway thing —well, I feel like a pothole in it. So help me sort this out. When I ask the computer for these two words, I'll find books about the Klondike trails, right?

MS. KYOKO: Well, Jarrod, it's not quite that simple. You see, you probably won't find a whole book about your "little" topic.

JARROD: Oh, yes, I keep forgetting! If I find a whole book on my topic, the topic is too big. Okay, so where does that leave me? How am I going to be able to use the computer catalog?

MS. KYOKO: Looking for materials takes a different thinking strategy than looking for topics.

JUAN: You guys won't have any trouble once you get started. You know, if you type in the wrong word and get 300 items, just cancel and try another word. The menus on screen are easy to follow. Just relax!

JARROD: Okay, Juan, I'll call on you when I get stuck! Meantime, I have another question.

SHONDRA: Oh, man. Jarrod, the big question mark!

JARROD: Yeah, that's me. Anyway, I read in the newspaper that there's a big centennial celebration to honor the Klondike gold rush. What if I want to find really up-to-date information about that? I won't find that in books.

MS. KYOKO: Good point. And you're right. You need a different kind of reference to find up-to-date information. It's another general reference, called **periodicals.**

COMPUTER HINT

When you are doing a computer search, think bigger. It's the opposite of looking for "little" topics. For instance, look for "Yukon Territory" if "Klondike" gives you nothing. Look for "birds" rather than "hawks." If your search shows nothing when you ask for "Harriet Tubman," then look for "Civil War" or "Underground Railroad."

Another advantage of many computer catalogs is their ability to print out a list of the references you want to locate. You don't have to copy everything by hand.

JARROD: You mean, like magazines and newspapers?

MS. KYOKO: Right.

JARROD: So how do I find articles without flipping through tons of magazines?

MS. KYOKO: To find periodical articles, you'll use a different search. The ***Readers' Guide to Periodical Literature,*** usually called the *Readers' Guide*, lists articles found in about 200 of the most popular magazines.

JUAN: Is that a computer search, too?

MS. KYOKO: That depends on your library.

COMPUTER HINT

In many libraries, the *Readers' Guide to Periodical Literature* is available on CD-ROM. So are other periodical indexes, like *Newsbank*. Some indexes give article titles. Some give article summaries. And some give complete articles on screen. Any of these can be printed out for take-home reading. Often, though, the more you can read on screen, the fewer periodicals are listed in the index.

Most CD-ROM references are updated monthly. Thus they are the most current. You search these references about the same way you search any other computerized index.

Online services also offer a wide variety of current resources. Check especially for online newspapers. They are more than newspapers on computer. They include details behind the stories that never appear in print.

JUAN: As far as I know, our school library has *Readers' Guide* only in book form, but those are such huge books. How do we use them?

MS. KYOKO: The organization is somewhat like that in the card catalog or computer catalog. Each article indexed in the *Readers' Guide* has two entries: **subject and author.** But not title. And just as you did for the card or computer catalog, you'll use subject entries most. Let's look at a sample page so I can show you what I mean.

MS. KYOKO: Look what you find in each entry. Now, where are my glasses? They're always disappearing. Okay, here we go. If the article has a by-line, you'll find the **author's name.** There's the **name of the article.** Then the **name of the magazine** where the article appears. And the **date** of the magazine.

SHONDRA: Those are easy enough. But what's that funny bunch of numbers?

MS. KYOKO: Ah, the numbers! Something like 81:17-21+. They're important. The first number, 81, is the magazine's **volume number.** That number helps you find the magazine on the library shelf or on microfilm. The numbers 17-21+ are the **page numbers** for the article.

JARROD: What's the little **plus sign?**

MS. KYOKO: The + sign means the article continues later in the magazine. Let's say you start reading on page 17. You get to the bottom of page 21, and there's a little note. It says "Continued on page 103." You find the rest of the article there. That's what the "plus" sign means.

JUAN: But Ms. K., there are some other odd-looking notes in some of these entries. What are they?

MS. KYOKO: Good question. You may see a series of notes that tell you the article has something extra. Like a map, an illustration, or a bibliography.

Author

Periodical title

Article title

Volume and page number

Date of publication (September, 1990)

Article about Westmore

Subdivision of subject

Includes map

Cross-reference

Author

Illustration included

Continuation of aticle on nonconsecutive pages

Clarification of article's subject

Subjects

Cross-reference

Illustration and portrait

Incudes bibliography and footnotes

WESTLAKE, MELVYN
Measuring 'human well-being'. *World Press Review* 37:67 S '90
WESTMORE, MICHAEL
about
Letting nature lead the way. M. Weisang. il por *theatre Crafts* 24:38-41+Ag/S '90
WESTWOOD (LOS ANGELES, CALIF.)
Los Angeles: Westwood, ho! C. Michener. il map *Travel Holiday* 173:22+ Jl '90
WETLANDS
Florida
See also
Everglades (Fla.)
Illinois
Green suits gray suits & white hats [environmental concerns of St. Louis District Army Corps of Engineers] J. Madson. il map *Audubon* 92:108-11 Jl '90
Lousiana
See also
Bayous
Landfill in the bayous [proposed site for New Orleans] C. L. Bankston, III. il *The Progressive* 54:13-14 Jl '90
Losing Louisiana. D. G. Schueler. il por map *Audubon* 92:78-87 Jl '90
Missouri
Green suits gray suits & white hats [environmental concerns of St. Louis District Army Corps of Engineers] J. Madson. il map *Audubon* 92:108-11 Jl '90
Nebraska
Some small blue places. J Madson. il *Audubon* 92:40-5 Jl '90
North Carolina
See also
Black River Swamp (N.C.)
Pennsylvania
The fable of Pozsgai's swamp [J. Pozsgai convicted of illegally filling a wetland] J. G. Mitchell. il por *Audubon* 92:112-14+ Jl '90
WETZSTEON, ROSS
A sod story. il *Sport (New York, N.Y.)* 81:68-71 Jl '90
WEXLER, TANYA
about
Bright stars at Yale. ill pors *Seventeen* 49:168-71 S '90
WEYERHAEUSER COMPANY
Weyerhaeuser's exports: an endangered species? [log sales] D. J. Yang. il *Business Week* p50-1 Jl 16 '90
WEYRICH, PAUL
Conservatism for the people. il *National Review* 42:24-7 S 3 '90
WFAN (NEW YORK, N.Y.: RADIO STATION) *See* Radio stations
WHALE TOOTH CARVING *See* Scrimshaw
WHALES
Romancing the whales [work of B. Beland with belugas of St. Lawrence River] B. Came. il por *Maclean's* 103:49 S 17 '90
WHALES, FOSSIL
Hind limbs of Eocene Basilosaurus: evidence of feet in whales. P. D. Gingerich and others. bibl f il *Science* 249:154-7 Jl 13 '90

76

UNDERSTANDING
A *READERS' GUIDE* ENTRY

Each *Readers' Guide* entry includes:

name of the article
author's name, if there is one
name of the **magazine** where article appears
issue of magazine (date, volume number, page
    number)
special features in the article, if any

JARROD: Seems like there are lots of strange abbreviations in the *Readers' Guide.* I don't understand what they mean.

MS. KYOKO: When you want to find what the **abbreviations** stand for, look inside the front cover of the *Readers' Guide.* All the abbreviations are listed there.

SHONDRA: One thing's for sure. If the *Readers' Guide* is for current stuff, I won't need to bother with it. That's one less headache for me.

MS. KYOKO: That's a logical conclusion, Shondra. But you know, I'd check anyway. Who knows? Maybe there's some reason for Harriet Tubman to have her name in current periodicals. You might find something exciting.

CRITICAL THINKING HINT

Think about your topic. Is it current, or is there something currently in the news about it? If so, look in periodicals. Otherwise, you will find your information in books.

Many topics, of course, will have information in both books and periodicals. Whenever possible, use a good balance of both.

SHONDRA: I guess looking in periodicals is worth a try. Anything's worth a try to get the information I need.

MS. KYOKO: That's a good way to look at it! Now there's one more area of the library I want to mention. That's the **vertical file.** Librarians keep all kinds of neat little things there. You'll find pamphlets, clippings, brochures, bulletins—little things. They're all in file folders in alphabetical order by subject.

JUAN: What topics will we find? Are there things about hawks?

MS. KYOKO: You never know. That's why you should always look there. Let's say, for instance, you're looking for something about Alzheimer's disease. If you look in the file folder marked "A," you might find a whole stack of bulletins from the Alzheimer's Association about the disease. There might even be one on how teenagers can cope with grandparents who are suffering from the disease. Vertical file. Easy to use. Maybe has great information; maybe not. But don't ignore it.

SHONDRA: Well, seems to me like we have quite a little job to do. General references. Books. Magazines and newspapers. Vertical file.

JARROD: Boy, this worries me. What with soccer practice and all, I'm going to be really busy.

MS. KYOKO: Yes, you'll be busy. But looking for resources is something like being a detective. You're looking for clues. Looking for details. Looking for connections between ideas. Looking for leads. I think that's what makes research fun. It's like solving a mystery! So, let's summarize what we've been talking about.

JUAN: You make the library search sound like more fun than I think it will be. But I have another question. What do we do when we find things—books, magazines, or whatever— listed in a catalog or index? Do we just go find it, check it out of the library, and haul it home?

MS. KYOKO: I'd suggest you glance through the books. Look at the table of contents. Look in the index. See if there's any-

Map of Library Research

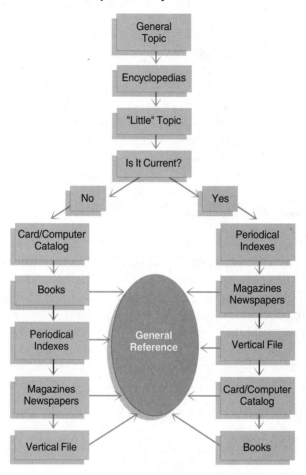

thing that refers to your "little" topic or to the items in your tentative list.

SHONDRA: Oh, that's right. I almost forgot about my list. I can use the list to find keywords in tables of contents and indexes.

MS. KYOKO: Right! So skim books and magazines before you take them all home. Some may not be useful. Better to find our earlier than later.

JARROD: So the only little job we have right now is finding books and magazines that seem to have helpful information. Is that right?

MS. KYOKO: Yes, but don't forget the other resources, too.

JUAN: You mean the auditory and visual stuff?

MS. KYOKO: Precisely. Now, let me get out of your way so you can get on with your search!

TIME MANAGEMENT GUIDELINES

Checking for resources in the library is clearly limited to the times the library is open. Make sure to schedule time with that in mind. Then make good use of your time. Don't visit, get distracted, or otherwise lose focus on your goal. You are there to find as much information on your topic as you can.

If your report is due in ...	finish your library search in ...
4 weeks	3 days
6 weeks	5 days
8 weeks	6 days
10 weeks	7 days

THREE STUDENTS' PROGRESS

As Shondra, Juan, and Jarrod began their searches, each made interesting discoveries. As you hear about them, you will learn more about researching.

SHONDRA: First I looked for books. I knew I'd find most of my information that way. The computer catalog gave me 31 entries including—and get this!—fiction, juvenile drama, and juvenile poetry. Those I could scratch right away. But you know what? All the other books on the list had a call number beginning 921 T 885. That told me exactly where to look for everything!

Next I decided to take Ms. K.'s advice and look through a periodical index. My library had *Readers' Guide* books and two CD-ROM indexes. I started with *Readers' Guide* and looked up "Tubman, Harriet." In the 1990 edition I finally found two articles.

When I found the two magazines, I learned that one had only a single-page article, but all of it about Tubman. I checked it out. The other had an article about the ten most unforgettable black women. Only a paragraph about Tubman. Nothing there I hadn't read before, but I made a photocopy and left the magazine.

Then the librarian suggested I use a CD-ROM index. It had the full articles on screen, so I didn't have to hunt up the magazine or newspaper. Actually, it was kind of fun. I used "Tubman, Harriet" for a keyword search and found ten articles! But, did I find some strange things!

One article told about a bank that prints Tubman's pictures on their checks. Another was about the Tubman Elementary School in Newark. Another talked about a nursing home named after Tubman. One was about Cicely Tyson's role in a movie titled *The Diary of Harriet Tubman*. I do wish I could see that movie. Ms. Kyoko said we could use visuals!

Anyway, what I learned was that a keyword search led me to all kinds of things that weren't really important to my "little" topic. I was a little put out. Felt that maybe I'd wasted time. Still, I learned about that movie.

JARROD: I know it wasn't Ms. K.'s advice, but I started my search in the general reference section. I needed to get my head on straight about location and stuff like that. I guess I'm a visual learner, but anyway I need to picture in my mind what I'm reading about. A couple of atlases had some good maps. And in the almanac I found that the whole Yukon Territory has only 27,700 people. Can you imagine that?

The almanac also showed that the Yukon has Canada's highest peak—Mt. Logan, at 19,850 feet. Now if that's where these gold seekers had to go through—well, this whole thing is just awesome. I also found out that the Yukon River is almost 2000 miles long. I'm already a little overwhelmed by size, distance, and lack of population in this Klondike area. It must be true wilderness. Even now.

Next I started looking for books. Juan, you'll be pleased to know I didn't have to ask for help. The computer catalog screens were pretty easy to follow. I noticed right away, though, that Pierre Berton was listed as the author of several books about the Klondike. So I did an author search and turned up a couple more. Actually I'm a little worried. I think I have too much material. I can't read all of these books. Soccer practice takes too much of my time to read six or eight whole books. I hope Ms. K. has some quick help for me!

JUAN: I really don't have much to add. I just hunted up "birds" in the catalog and pulled the books. Ms. K.'s advice paid off. You remember, the part about looking on the shelves near where we found books? Well, sure enough I did find books on the shelf that I hadn't found in the catalog. In every book the index told me not only that red-tailed hawks were included but gave me the page or two I needed. One book didn't have an index, so I just didn't bother with it. In most cases, I just made photocopies of the pages and left the books in the library. This is going to be a snap!

JARROD: I hope you followed Ms. K.'s other advice. Did you make a note of the book title and author of those photocopied pages?

JUAN: Oops. I forgot that. Oh, well, we'll see.

TIPS AND TRAPS

You have already heard from Shondra, Juan, and Jarrod about their experiences in their own searches. Now listen to Ms. Dewey, the librarian.

MS. DEWEY: We librarians have one main job: to help people find what they need. Four kinds of students make our jobs really hard. I hope you're not one of these four!

First are the students who seem afraid to ask for any kind of help. They just muddle and fumble around and then whine to their friends that they "can't find anything." We never hear from them, so we can never help them.

Second are the students who say they need help finding things but can't tell us what they need. They say they need "something about wetlands" or "something about the Civil War." You need to ask clear questions about specific problems. Make specific requests. Like "I need books about the Underground Railroad, and I need help finding card catalog headings." Or "What should I use in a subject search if I want a magazine article about former President Carter's work with Habitat for Humanity?" Tell us what you need, and we can help you find it.

Third are students who expect us librarians to do everything for them. They seem to take the do-it-for-me attitude instead of the show-me-how-to-do-it attitude. You must learn to do your own search. But when you're stumped, then ask us to show you how.

Fourth are a few students who call their neighborhood libraries and ask for "everything you have" on a topic. Forget it! We help, but we can't do all of your work for you. There are just too many of you! And don't send your mother to do your search, either.

CHECKLIST

You should be able to answer "yes" to the following questions about your detective work.

1. Have I checked general references like encyclopedias, almanacs, atlases?
2. Have I checked the card catalog or computer catalog for books on my topic?
   a. Have I looked up headings bigger than my "little" topic?
   b. Have I looked for other books by authors I already know about?
3. Have I checked periodical indexes for magazine and newspaper articles on my topic?
4. Have I considered non-book media, like pamphlets, films, audio-visual references?
5. Have I considered other sources, like museums, interviews, surveys, or experiments?

EXERCISES

Exercise A: Finding Sources

Directions: To complete this exercise, you will need to go to the library. Look for information about each of the items below. Tell whether you found the information easiest and most quickly in General Reference (Gen Ref), Card or Computer Catalog (Cat), or Periodical Indexes (Per Ind).

Cooperative Activity: If your teacher agrees, work in a cooperative group to complete this activity.

1. Description of how to access a computer bulletin board
2. Brief biography of Earvin "Magic" Johnson
3. Names of candidates in the upcoming national election
4. Review of new computer software
5. List of Pulitzer Prize winners in Journalism
6. A map of the solar system
7. Photographs from the Hubble Space Telescope
8. Poetry by Langston Hughes
9. Source of the phrase "Give me liberty or give me death!"
10. History of aviation

Exercise B: Using General References

Directions: Much information can be found in general reference sources like **dictionaries, encyclopedias, indexes, yearbooks, almanacs, biographical dictionaries, atlases, and periodicals.** Each of the items below can be found in some general reference. Where would you look for each of these? Use your library's general reference section to find out.

Cooperative Activity: If your teacher agrees, work in cooperative groups to complete this activity.

1. A list of newspaper articles about lawn mower accidents
2. The number of people of Hispanic origin in Milwaukee, Wisconsin
3. A few sentences that explain who Nelson Mandela is
4. A detailed article about Indira Gandhi
5. Quotations about honesty
6. A map showing the location of mountains in Alaska
7. A list of magazine articles about Larry Bird
8. An article about Charlie Ward of Florida State winning the Heisman Trophy
9. 1992 legislation affecting school newspapers
10. A list of the world's ten largest cities

Exercise C: Understanding the *Readers' Guide*

Directions: Use the *Readers' Guide* excerpt on page 76 to answer these questions.

1. Instead of "Whale Tooth Carving," under what heading should readers look?
2. Name three other cross-references for "Wetlands."
3. What is the title of the article about Michael Westmore?
4. In what periodical is there an article about Tanya Wexler?
5. Which issue of *Business Week* includes an article about Weyerhaeuser Company?
6. What do the numbers 42:24-7 refer to in the subject entry "Weyrich, Paul"?
7. What does the + refer to in the numbers 92:112-14+? (See the "Pennsylvania" subdivision under "Wetlands.")
8. Who wrote the article about Illinois wetlands?
9. Which three articles include maps?
10. Which article includes a bibliography?
11. Who wrote the first article listed, "Measuring Human Well-Being"?
12. For the article in the "Pennsylvania" subdivision under "Wetlands," what is the information in brackets: [J. Pozsgai convicted of illegally filling a wetland]?

Exercise D: Understanding the Catalog

Directions: Use the author card on page 69 to answer the following questions.

1. Who is the author of the book described on this card?
2. What is the book about?
3. How many pages are in this book?
4. Are there any illustrations in this book?
5. When was the book published?
6. Name three other subject headings where this book is listed.

7. Why would it be important for a student to check the subject headings if he has already found this author card?
8. What does this book include that is helpful to someone doing a research report?

Exercise E: Now You Write

Directions: Answer the following questions about your own search for information.

1. Which general references did you check?
2. Which general references had useful information about your topic?
3. When you checked the card or computer catalog, under what headings did you look?
4. Under which of these headings did you find books on your topic?
5. When you checked a periodical index, under what headings did you look?
6. Under which of these headings did you find magazines for your topic?
7. When you checked the vertical file, under what headings did you look?
8. Under which of these headings did you find information useful for your topic?
9. Where else did you look for information?
10. What useful information did you find outside the library?

PEER EDITING GUIDELINES

When you finish Exercise E, ask a peer editor or someone in your writing group to think through your answers with you. He or she should use the following questions to respond.

1. After I read about your search in the general references, I think you could also look . . . to find . . .

2. After I read about your search in the catalog, I think you could also look under other headings like . . .
3. After I read about your search in the periodical index, I think you could also look under other headings like . . .
4. After I read about where you searched outside the library, I think you could also find information . . .

PORTFOLIO POINTERS

When you finish Exercise E and your peer editor responds to your search results, put both papers in your portfolio. Then answer these questions.

1. With which part of the search do I feel I did the best job? Why?
2. Which part of the search was hardest for me? Why?
3. What did I learn about library searches (general references, catalogs, indexes, vertical files)?
4. What did I learn about searching outside the library?
5. Do I need to search any parts of the library again? If so, which ones?

Chapter 5
Preparing Bibliography Cards

Y ou have been to the library and checked out sources. You have books, magazines, pamphlets, and possibly other materials. Perhaps you have also planned to use other resources, such as interviews. For the most part, though, you will tap these other resources after you have finished your basic research. Now you're ready for your next little job.

MS. KYOKO: This little job is really easy. You'll be making a 3" × 5" card for each of your books, magazines, or other sources. We call these little cards **bibliography cards,** or "bib cards" for short.

SHONDRA: Bibliography? The name sounds scary. What's it mean?

MS. KYOKO: "Bibliography" is just a fancy word for "list of sources."

JARROD: I don't mean to sound rude, Ms. K., but isn't writing out these cards kind of silly? After all, I have the books and stuff. Why do I need to make a card for each one?

MS. KYOKO: Sure, you have the sources. But there are good reasons for making a card for each one. First, your books will be due at the library before your final project is finished.

JUAN: Wait a minute. So they're due. We can renew them.

MS. KYOKO: Point well taken, Juan. So, let me give you the rest of the story. Two things. First, you'll be writing about what you learn from your sources—like how a hawk hunts. Or how Harriet Tubman survived. Or how people reached the Klondike. Your audience wonders how you know these things. To tell them, you'll have to write little notes. We'll talk later about how. So that's the first point.

JUAN: And the second point?

MS. KYOKO: Second point. At the end of your project you will do something called a **Works Cited list.** That's a list of all the sources you used for your project.

SHONDRA: So we're really starting that list now? Is that what these cards are all about?

MS. KYOKO: That's the idea.

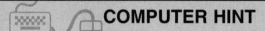

COMPUTER HINT

You can make your bibliography "cards" on your word processor. You may want to put information in alphabetical order as you enter it.

Be sure to make a new file for your bib list. You could call it "bib" or "works."

When you have entered the details, save the file. And print a copy so you can use it when you take notes.

Remember to make a backup file!

JARROD: As usual, I'm still confused. What's the connection between bib cards and the little notes and lists? Seems to me if we have the books and stuff, we don't need a bunch of cards that lists them all.

MS. KYOKO: In a way that's true, Jarrod. But we're also going to use the cards for some shortcuts later.

JARROD: Now you're talking my language. I'm all for shortcuts!

MS. KYOKO: I thought you'd like that! So think of these cards as an easy way to keep track of whole books. You're going to have to trust me a little on this one. I don't want to start talking now about notes and other little jobs that come up later. We want to keep this in simple, little steps.

JUAN: Okay, we'll trust you. Let's get down to business. What do we put on these cards?

MS. KYOKO: Basic information. Titles. Authors. Where the things were published. Who published them, and when. Just the basics.

JUAN: I have some books I probably won't use. So I don't need to make a card for them, right?

MS. KYOKO: I'd make a card for every book, magazine, tape, pamphlet, map, or cassette I found. You can suffer a lot of grief when you don't have all the details about a source.

JUAN: You know, now that you mention it, I think I'm already in trouble. I found books that had only a few pages about red-tails. I know you said not to do this, but I photocopied the pages and left the books. Is that a problem?

MS. KYOKO: Oh, dear. It could be. You didn't write the titles of the books on the photocopies?

JUAN: No. But I think I can figure it out. I'll have to look through all the books again.

JARROD: Good luck, Juan. I think Ms. K. is being nice. Even I can see you're headed back to the library!

MS. KYOKO: Jarrod's right, Juan. At least you're finding out sooner rather than later. Since you copied those pages just yesterday, chances are good that you'll find the books again quickly.

JUAN: You're probably right. Boy! Leave it to me to mess up so early in the game.

MS. KYOKO: It's no crisis, Juan. That's why we're doing this one little job at a time!

SHONDRA: Ms. K., could you give us an example of a bib card? Here's a book I found on Harriet Tubman. Show us what the card should look like.

MS. KYOKO: Thanks, Shondra. Glasses? Okay, here they are. Ah, this looks like a good book. Good index in the back, too. Okay. Let's use your book as an example, Shondra. We'll write three groups of words that you can think of as "sentences."

CRITICAL THINKING HINT

Think of the bibliography card as a "paragraph" with three "sentences." Put a period at the end of each sentence.

SHONDRA: This sounds easier all the time. What do you mean by "sentences"?

MS. KYOKO: Well, of course these aren't really sentences with subjects and verbs. They're only groups of words. But if you think of them as "sentences," you'll remember how to write them.

JARROD: That seems helpful. What's the first "sentence"?

MS. KYOKO: The first is the **author's name.** Put her last name first, a comma, and then her first. And remember to put a period at the end of the "sentence." Like this:

Ferris, Jeri.

SHONDRA: That's a snap. What's the second "sentence"?

MS. KYOKO: It's just as easy. The second "sentence" is the **title.** Be sure to underline titles.

JARROD: I'm always messing up titles. I thought you put quotation marks around titles.

MS. KYOKO: In general, you underline titles of big things and put quotation marks around titles of little things. So underline book titles, and put quotation marks around book chapter titles. Underline magazine titles, and put quotation marks around magazine article titles.

SHONDRA: That's logical.

MS. KYOKO: Most rules have some logic somewhere. That includes the rules for capitalization. Be sure to capitalize titles correctly. Always capitalize the first and last words of a title. Capitalize all other words except little ones. Like articles (*a, an,* and *the*). And prepositions (like *of, by, between, along,* and so forth).

JUAN: Aren't there a lot of prepositions?

MS. KYOKO: Yes. You should check your grammar handbook for a complete list.

SHONDRA: Is that it, then, for this second "sentence"?

MS. KYOKO: One more thing. Put a period at the end of the "sentence." So it looks like this:

Go Free or Die: A Story about Harriet Tubman.

JUAN: So far, so good. What's the third "sentence"?

MS. KYOKO: The third "sentence" gives the **publishing details.** Three details. City, publisher, and date. Look, here's where you find it. Right after the title page. You want the **city** where the book was published. In this case, it's Minneapolis. Then the **publisher.** That's Carolrhoda Books, Inc. And then the **date** it was published. Let's see. Here it is near the bottom of the page—1988. So write all that in a "sentence" like this:

Minneapolis: Carolrhoda Books, Inc., 1988.

Be sure to notice the unusual puctuation. There's a colon after the city and a comma between the publisher and the date.

JARROD: That's it? Just three little groups of words?

MS. KYOKO: Three little groups. Any questions?

JUAN: Several of my books have more than one author. Do I list all their names?

MS. KYOKO: List up to three names. If there are more than three, list only the first. Then say "and others." Let's see one of your books. Okay, this one has three authors. Write their names like this:

Ehrlich, Paul R., David S. Dobkin, and Darryl Wheye.

JUAN: So I list last name first only with the first author. The rest are in natural order. Why?

MS. KYOKO: You'll alphabetize by the first author named, so the others can be in natural order.

JUAN: That makes sense.

MS. KYOKO: Now, Juan, here's a book in your stack that has four editors, not authors. You'll use a little abbreviation after their names to show that they are editors, like this:

Pearson, T. Gilbert, and others, eds.

SHONDRA: I can do this! Just three little groups of words!

Three Parts to Bibliography Cards for Books

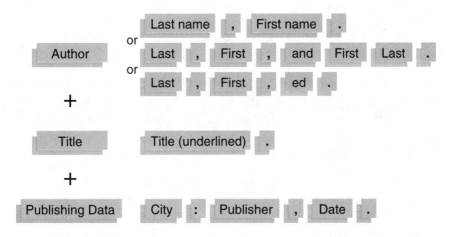

JUAN: Three little "sentences"! So, as you said, Ms. K., we should think of each group of three as sort of like a paragraph?

MS. KYOKO: In a way, Juan. Only when you write this "paragraph," don't indent the first line. Instead, indent everything *but* the first line. That's correct form.

JUAN: You said most rules were logical. So why such a form?

MS. KYOKO: There is a reason. Later, you'll list your sources in alphabetical order. If you move the first line to the left, you'll make the job easier. By the way, we call that **hanging indentation.**

JARROD: No problem. So that's it, right?

MS. KYOKO: That's all you *have* to do. Personally, I like to add two other things. First, I write the book's call number in the corner of the card.

JARROD: Why do that? I've already found the book by its call number.

MS. KYOKO: True. But as soon as you finish with a book, you'll probably take it back to the library. You'll get tired of books piled everywhere and filling up your locker. If you put the call number on the bib card, you can find it again quickly if you need to.

JARROD: Good idea. Call number. You said, though, there were two things. What's the other?

MS. KYOKO: Any little note that will help me remember the book. Like your book, Shondra. It has a really good index. I'd note that on the bottom of the card. Or if it has good maps or good pictures, I'd make a note of that. Or if there's only one really good chapter, I'd say that, too.

JARROD: Do we always have to write these little notes?

MS. KYOKO: No. Just if there's something you want to remember about the book.

SHONDRA: Okay, I wrote this card while you were talking. Is it right?

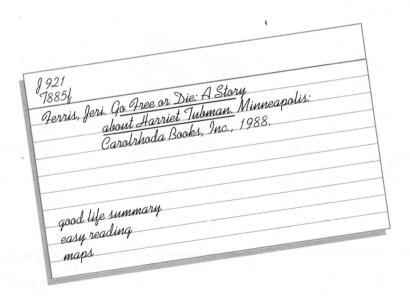

MS. KYOKO: Yes! See how the hanging indentation makes it easy to see "Ferris"? That's the word you'll use later to put the cards in alphabetical order.

SHONDRA: Okay, good. Now here's a magazine I found. Do I do the same thing for a **magazine card?**

MS. KYOKO: In general, yes. But the third "sentence" is different. As you know, a magazine is a series of articles. As a result, you have two titles to deal with. The title of the magazine and the title of the article. One of the three "sentences" names the article.

SHONDRA: Run that by me again. I didn't follow.

MS. KYOKO: Here's how it works. The first little "sentence" is the author of the article. The second is the name of the article. The third is the name of the magazine, the date, and page number or numbers. Here's what the last "sentence" looks like:

<u>National Geographic</u> Mar. 1996: 189-194.

SHONDRA: That looks funny. So, let's see. There's no punctuation after the name of the magazine. I use the abbreviation for the month. I put a colon after the year. And a hyphen shows more than one page. Right?

MS. KYOKO: Right! Sometimes a magazine article starts on one page and continues further back. In that case, just use the plus sign (+) instead of listing all the pages, like this:

<u>Southern Living</u> Sept. 1996: 84+.

JARROD: What about a **newspaper?** Is it like a magazine?

MS. KYOKO: Yes. Same situation. You have a newspaper title and an article title.

Three Parts to Bibliography Cards for Periodicals

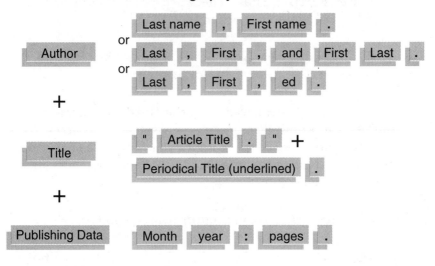

CRITICAL THINKING HINT

Think about the purpose of a bibliography card. It tells you—and later, your audience—where you found facts and details. To meet that purpose, you need the three parts: title, author, and publishing data. For periodicals, readers need to know two titles: the newspaper or magazine title and the article title. Thinking about the purpose will help you get the right details on the bib cards.

SHONDRA: This all looks pretty easy. Here's one of my magazine cards. Is it okay?

MS. KYOKO: Perfect! You have the title of the article in quotation marks. The period is inside the quotation marks. You have the title of the magazine underlined. The date is abbreviated, followed by a colon. Then the page numbers.

> Norment, Lynn. "Ten Most Unforgettable
> Black Women." *Ebony* Feb. 1990: 104+.
>
> only a little about H. T.
> good comparison w/other 9

SHONDRA: Great. But, now I have a problem with this other magazine. There's **no author.** What do I write instead of the author's name?

MS. KYOKO: Nothing. Just start with the title of the article.

SHONDRA: Ummmm. Like this?

> "First Woman to Lead U. S. Troops Was Black,
> Not White." *Jet* 23 Jan. 1990: 18.

MS. KYOKO: Right! See! It's easy. Any other questions?

JARROD: What about the **encyclopedia articles** we have? Are they any different?

MS. KYOKO: Same idea. Remember, you just want all the details that will let you—or your audience—find the same article, same book, same page, whatever. For an encyclopedia article, give the article title, the name of the encyclopedia, and the date. Let's see you try that, Jarrod.

JARROD: What about a page number? You didn't mention that.

MS. KYOKO: When materials are alphabetical, as in a dictionary or an encyclopedia, you don't need a page number.

JARROD: Okay. This entry should be easy. How's this?

"Klondike." *Encyclopedia Americana.* 1993.

MS. KYOKO: Perfect. You have the period inside the quotation marks. The date is all that's necessary because encyclopedias are so well known.

SHONDRA: I have another question. I found some information on CD-ROM. Do I have to have a CD-ROM bib card, too?

MS. KYOKO: Yes, Shondra, you'll need a card for every source. In short, just put in whatever someone else needs to find the same information you found. Tell me about the CD-ROM program you were using, Shondra.

SHONDRA: I was using the SIRS Researcher. I entered "Tubman, Harriet" and it sent me to the category "Women." I found this article and printed it out.

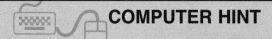 **COMPUTER HINT**

To make a bibliography card for sources from computers, follow these suggestions:

Give the same details as for books and periodicals, but add the data source and identifying number, if any. See these examples:

Article without author
"Computers in Education." *Facts on File News Digest*. New York: Facts on File, Inc., 1988. CD-ROM.

Article with author
Rosenberg, Victor. "Computers." *The New Grolier Electronic Encyclopedia*. Danbury, CT: Grolier Electronic Publishing, Inc., 1988. CD-ROM.

Newspaper article with author
Booth, William. "Rebuilding Wetlands: Nature Proves a Tough Act to Follow." *Washington [D.C.] Post* 30 Jan. 1990. Newsbank ENV 5:C13-14.

MS. KYOKO: Great! Look what you have. It's an article from the *Washington Monthly*, so you'll do a card for a periodical. Now, add the part about the CD-ROM you were using.

Boo, Katherine. "The Organization Woman." *Washington Monthly.* Dec. 1991: 44+. SIRS Researcher. "Women." 4: 60.

SHONDRA: The only thing new here is what comes after the page number. "SIRS Researcher" is the name of the CD-ROM program. "Women" is the section where I found the article. And "4: 60" is like a page number that shows where this article is on the CD-ROM.

JUAN: You know, there's a pattern to all this. We do author, title, and publishing details. Tell the reader exactly where to find what we've found.

MS. KYOKO: Juan, you summarized it perfectly. Let me leave you with this list of examples, and you can finish your bibliography cards quickly!

Books

Book by single author Degmann, Sylvester. <u>Fresh-Water Biology</u>. New York: Alfred A. Knopf, 1992.

Book by two or three authors   Cousteau, Jacques-Yves, and Philippe Diole. <u>Life and Death in a Coral Sea</u>. Garden City, NY: Doubleday and Company, Inc., 1971.

Book by four or more authors   Porter, Roy E., and others. <u>The Writer's Manual</u>. Palm Springs: ETC Publications, 1991.

Book with an editor or editors   Polking, Kirk, Joan Bloss, and Colleen Cannon, eds. <u>Writer's Encyclopedia</u>. Cincinnati: Writer's Digest Books, 1993.

Article in an encyclopedia or other reference book "Steinbeck, John." <u>Contemporary Authors</u>. 1968 ed.

Magazines

Article from a monthly periodical   Alva, Walter. "The Moche of Ancient Peru: New Tomb of Royal Splendor." <u>National Geographic</u> June 1990: 2-15.

Article from a weekly or biweekly periodical   Cahan, V., and C. Blank. "The Good Earth May Get Even Harder to Till." <u>Business Week</u> 4 June 1990: 140-141.

Article with no author named   "Sheep's Best Friend." <u>Harrowsmith</u> Mar.-Apr. 1990: 117.

Newspapers

Article with author in daily paper   Ashley, Doris. "Don't Presume Justice." <u>The Miami Herald</u> 25 Mar. 1995, Final ed.: B2.

Article without author in quarterly paper   "Save Vanishing Rain Forests." <u>The Indiana Sierran</u> Spring 1995: 4.

Other Print and Nonprint Resources

Pamphlet   <u>Wetlands: Indiana's Endangered Natural Resource</u>. Indianapolis, IN: Indiana Department of Natural Resources, 1996.

Radio or television program <u>Latest Edition</u>. Writ. Leslie Nunsuch. PBS. WJXT, Princeton 14 Aug. 1990.

Letter, E-Mail communication, or public online posting Stallings, Karen. Letter to the author. 4 July 1996.

Interview Muldoon, Bridgette. Personal interview. 27 Sept. 1995.

Map or chart <u>Canada</u>. Map. Chicago: Rand McNally, 1988.

Lecture, speech, or address Gillespie, Marcia Ann. Address. Opening General Sess. Friends of the Wilderness Spring Conference. Lexington. 15 June 1996.

TIME MANAGEMENT GUIDELINES

Make a bibliography card as soon as you find each source. As a result, no matter how long you have to do your research report, you should finish your bib cards quickly.

If your report is due in . . .	finish your bibliography cards in . . .
4 weeks	1 day
6 weeks	1 day
8 weeks	2 days
10 weeks	2 days

THREE STUDENTS' PROGRESS

The bibliography cards take very little time. They do, however, need your eye for detail. Writing them correctly now will help you do a good job on the list of sources you will later put in your final report. Listen to Shondra, Juan, and Jarrod talk about their experiences.

SHONDRA: I had a whole package of a hundred 3" × 5" cards—far more than I needed! After all, probably nobody needs more than 25 cards even after we throw some away. So four of us shared the package. Actually I used seventeen. That includes the card Ms. Kyoko helped me with for the CD-ROM program.

JUAN: You guys remember that problem I had? I'd made photocopies of pages without checking out the books. Well, I went back to the library to find the books. And guess what? Somebody had already checked them out. When I talked to Ms. Dewey, though, she said to check the computer catalog. She said the catalog would have what I need if I recognized the book titles. Lucky for me, the photocopies showed the page numbers. So I got what I needed. That was a break. With that I have twelve cards.

JARROD: For a change, I think even I have this under control. I have a card for each book I've found. Even though I didn't find any magazine articles, I did find a video. Ms. Kyoko said to use the same form as for a television program, so I have that card finished, too. So I have sixteen cards. I'm not sure I'll find something on my "little" topic in all of them, but they all have stuff about the Klondike.

SHONDRA: I'm just worried about all the details. One of my friends did her report last year and wasted all kinds of time. Basically, she was careless. She left off dates or page numbers or volume numbers. Then she had to go back to the library twice just to hunt up those things. Of course, she had the same problem you did, Juan. The books were already checked out again.

Maybe we could check each other's cards. You know, use the list the Ms. Kyoko gave us. If we catch problems now, we'll save hours later. What do you say?

JARROD: I'd love it. You know how I am. This just isn't my thing.

JUAN: In spite of the little trap I got caught in, I do have a good eye for detail. Let's do it. I'll check yours and you check mine. Among us we can spot any problems.

TIPS AND TRAPS

Three quick hints should do:

Use ink. Pencil tends to smear. Even if you have to cross out something or throw away an occasional card, you'll be better off in the long run using ink.

List only one source on a card. Since you will later put the sources in alphabetical order, you need a separate card for each.

Finally, check details carefully. Make sure you have all the information you need. Then check for spelling, capitalization, and punctuation.

CHECKLIST

You should be able to answer "yes" to each of the following questions.

1. Did I begin the first line of the bibliography card at the left margin?

2. Did I indent all other lines of the card?

3. If there is an **author,** did I list his or her name in reverse order, that is, last name first?

4. If there is no author, did I begin with the title?

5. Have I listed **titles** correctly?
   a. Did I underline titles of books and periodicals?
   b. Did I put quotation marks around titles of articles?
   c. Did I capitalize the correct words in titles?

6. Did I include all the publishing information for **books?**
   a. Did I list the city where the book was published?
   b. If the city is not well known, did I also give the state, abbreviated?
   c. Did I use a colon after I named the city?
   d. After the colon and a space, did I name the publisher?
   e. Did I put a comma after the name of the publisher?
   f. Did I give the publishing date?

7. Did I include all the publishing information for **magazines?**
   a. After the title of the magazine, did I give its date?
   b. Did I give the date in day-month-year order?
   c. Did I abbreviate the name of the month?
   d. Did I use a colon after the date, then a space, and then the page number?

8. Have I used periods in the right places?
   a. Did I use a period after author name(s)?
   b. Did I use a period after an article title or book title?
   c. Did I use a period at the end?
   d. Did I omit a period after a magazine title?

9. Did I add any notes to help me later, such as call numbers or special features?

EXERCISES

Exercise A: Revising Bibliography Entries

Directions: These bibliography entries have many errors in punctuation, capitalization, and form. Rewrite them correctly.

"Looking at Harriet Tubman, role model. Jet, pp 14-18+. August 1983.

Lynn Norment. Ten most unforgettable Black women. Ebony. February 1990, pp. 104, 106, 108.

T. Gilbert Pearson, and others, editors, *Birds of America*, 1917. Garden City Books, Garden City, N.Y.

Ripper, Charles L.. *Hawks*. William Morrow & Company. New York, 1956.

Harriet Tubman. Collier's Encyclopedia. Volume 22, page 505. New York, 1994.

Wallig, Gaird, A red-tailed hawk named Bucket, 1980, Millbrae, CA. Celestial arts.

"Yukon Passage", National Geographic Society. 1968, June: 118-127.

Exercise B: Preparing Bibliography Cards

Directions: Use the following information to prepare five bibliography cards. Use accurate form.

Jarrod has two sources on the Klondike. The first is a book by Pierre Berton. It is titled *Klondike: The Last Great Gold Rush 1896-1899*, published in 1972 by Penguin Books in Toronto. The other source is on CD-ROM from *The New Grolier Electronic Encyclopedia*. It was published in Danbury, Connecticut, in 1988 by Grolier Electronic Publishing, Inc. The article is "Klondike Gold Rush." No author is given.

Shondra found three magazine articles. One has no author listed. It is in the November 1988 issue of *Ebony* (pages 62, 66, and 68) and titled "Black Women in History." The other two articles are both in the July 1990 issue of *Jet* magazine. One, by Peter Murphy, is "Number One Spy" on pages 18-21. The other, "Symbols of the Woman's Role," is by Georgette Reiss on pages 42-43.

Exercise C: Now You Write

Directions: Make five bibliography cards of your own. If possible, write two for books, two for magazine articles, and one for some other source (like a newspaper, pamphlet, video, interview, encyclopedia, etc.). See the Checklist on pages 106–107 to remind you of mechanical details.

Peer Editing Guidelines

When you have finished Exercise C above, have a peer editor or someone from your writing group check your work. He or she should use the Checklist on pages 106–107 as a guide.

Portfolio Pointers

When you have finished your bibliography cards, put them in your portfolio. Then answer these questions.

1. What was the easiest part about writing bibliography cards?
2. What problems did I solve after my peer editor responded to my work?
3. What did I learn from writing the bibliography cards?
4. How can I apply what I learned to the rest of my work on my research report?

Chapter 6

Taking Notes

You've completed another little job. You have sources and a bibliography card for each of them. You should have about fifteen. Some of your sources will be more helpful than others. Some may even prove useless. That is all part of the process. You do a great deal of detective work during the research process. Some leads just do not pan out. On the other hand, some leads really open up and give you more than you expected.

At this point, then, you are ready to delve into your sources. You are ready for the next little job.

MS. KYOKO: Taking notes is your next little job. You've scouted the library for good sources. You have bibliography cards. Now you're ready to search your sources for information on your "little" topic.

JARROD: I think I get the idea. We're going to read all this stuff we found in the library and then do a report about what we read. That's the research report, right?

MS. KYOKO: In general, yes.

SHONDRA: Wait, wait, wait! Wait a minute! Read all this stuff? I have a stack of eight or ten books. I can't read all of them!

MS. KYOKO: Of course not. Remember the list, the tentative plan, you did earlier?

JUAN: Sure. We all have that.

MS. KYOKO: Good. It's your guide. Remember I said earlier that the plan would save you time later? Well, it's payoff time! Your plan will tell you which parts of a book to read.

SHONDRA: How does that work?

MS. KYOKO: Well, let's look at an example. Shondra, what did you list in your tentative plan?

SHONDRA: Here, let me show you.

MS. KYOKO: Okay, you have

escaped slavery
parents/family/friends/neighbors rescued
conductor of Underground Railroad
no education?
preparation for military
military life later
clever actions
worked with abolitionists

Now, as you read, you should look only for these ideas.

SHONDRA: Okay. So I look for just what's on my list. How do I keep from reading the whole book to find these things?

MS. KYOKO: Several ways. Check the **table of contents.** That will show which parts of the book will likely be most helpful. Look at **chapter headings and subheadings.** They zoom in on the book's main ideas. Look in the **index.** Check it for key words. **Skim** the text for key words. If you're looking for names, they'll jump out as you skim. Study **charts,**

graphs, illustrations, maps. They show ideas from the text. Find pages that seem to have details about your plan. Then read carefully. Those are the only pages you need to read.

**FINDING WHAT YOU NEED
(WITHOUT READING THE WHOLE BOOK)**

Check the table of contents.
Survey chapter headings and subheadings.
Look in the index.
Skim for key words.
Study charts, graphs, illustrations, maps.
Read carefully only those pages about your "little" topic.

SHONDRA: You know, this is starting to make sense. Now what's this part about taking notes?

MS. KYOKO: As you read, you'll take notes on **note cards.**

SHONDRA: More cards? I should have kept my package of 100 cards instead of sharing. Now I'll have to get more.

MS. KYOKO: No, Shondra, you did the right thing to share. It's true you'll need more cards. But these should be different from the ones you used for your bibliography cards. You might want a different color or a different size.

JUAN: Sorry, Ms. K., but you know I'm going to ask why.

MS. KYOKO: [*Laughing.*] I expected you to, Juan! Use a different color or size to keep from getting note cards and bib cards mixed up. Most students like a different size, usually 4" × 6". The larger size gives more room for notes. Of course, just because you use larger cards doesn't mean you have to fill them all! They're just easier to use and easier to read.

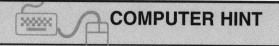

COMPUTER HINT

Some computer supply stores stock note-card-size perforated printer paper. To print your notes in the smaller space, adjust the right margin on your word processing software. Adjust the page length or use the return key to start a new note.

If you can't find the paper, space notes so that a standard 8 1/2" x 11" paper will accept three or four notes. Use the line guide on your screen to figure out spacing. So that you can sort and organize your notes later, cut the page into separate notes after it leaves the printer.

MS. KYOKO: Oh, and use ink for the same reason as before. Pencil smears. After you handle the cards a few times, you won't be able to read what you wrote. And write on only one side of the card. Above all—and this is important—put only one idea from one source on each note card.

> Put only one idea from one source on each note card.

SHONDRA: If we do that, it means we may have just a few words or only one sentence on this big 4" × 6" card. We leave the rest of the card blank?

MS. KYOKO: That's right. Of course, sometimes one idea from one source fills up a card. That's okay, too. It's important, though, to have only one idea from one book or one idea from one magazine on a card. Otherwise you'll have trouble organizing your cards later.

JUAN: What's this about "organizing your cards"?

MS. KYOKO: I don't want to get ahead of the game and confuse you. In short, though, remember that note cards are tiny parts of your report. After you finish your notes, you'll put them in a logical order. That's how you'll organize your material. But more about that later.

CRITICAL THINKING HINT

Think of note cards this way: They are like tiny parts of your paper. When you finish your note cards, your report is all but finished. If you take good, clear notes, it's easy to complete the paper or whatever form you have chosen for your report.

MS. KYOKO: Because these note cards are tiny parts of your paper, you want to do them carefully. The first thing you should do is **number** all your bibliography cards.

JUAN: Excuse me for being such a pest again, but why are we doing this?

MS. KYOKO: It's not being pesky to want to understand "why" about anything, Juan! In fact, you have a good question. We're numbering the cards to create a little code to identify sources.

JUAN: Ah, part of solving the mystery of all this!

MS. KYOKO: Right! Put the number in the upper right corner. You can begin with the number one, or any number you want. Then number the rest in order.

JARROD: So when we find something in a source that we want to use in our reports, we just copy it on a note card. Is that the idea?

MS. KYOKO: Yes and no. Yes, you'll put on a note card anything you find that you want to use. But no, you won't just copy it out of the source. Mostly you will put the ideas in your own words.

SHONDRA: Why not just copy it? That way the words will be right.

MS. KYOKO: Your audience wants to hear your voice, not that of the authors you're reading. You need to think about what these authors are saying. Then put their ideas into your words.

SHONDRA: I've heard teachers say that before, but it's hard for me. I'd rather just copy it and get on with it.

MS. KYOKO: I understand what you're saying. So let me help you. Do you have something here about Harriet Tubman?

SHONDRA: Sure, here's a copy of an encyclopedia article.

MS. KYOKO: Good. Let's look at part of this as an example. My glasses. I just had them.

SHONDRA: They're pushed up in your hair, Ms. K.

MS. KYOKO: Ah. Okay now, let's see the article you have.

Passage

Once free, Harriet joined the Abolitionist cause and soon decided to become a conductor on the Underground Railroad—the secret organization that aided southern slaves in their flight to freedom. Over the next ten years she made at least 15 expeditions into Maryland and personally escorted more that 200 runaway slaves to the North. Undeterred by the large rewards offered for her capture, she appeared to have something of a sixth sense in finding food and secure shelter during these hazardous missions and never lost any of her charges. Among slaves she came to be know as Moses, and she served as an inspiration to Abolitionists, white and black alike, including John Brown, who gave her the title "General Tubman."

from "Tubman, Harriet." *Collier's Encyclopedia.* 1994.

MS. KYOKO: Now, Shondra. There's no way you'd want to copy all that onto a note card. You can condense what's here into a few sentences of your own.

SHONDRA: That's where I start having trouble. It just seems so well-said here. I can't say it any better.

MS. KYOKO: Maybe you can't say it better. But you can say it in fewer words. Without looking at this copy, Shondra, tell me what this passage says.

CRITICAL THINKING HINT

When you get ready to write a note card, think of it as a summary. Put the idea of a paragraph into one sentence. That's the main idea. After you get the main idea, think about one or two ways the author explains it. Jot these down in your own words.

SHONDRA: Ummm. Well, it says that Tubman started working with the Abolitionists as soon as she was free. She freed about 200 other slaves and took them north. People were amazed at how she could find food and places for the runaways to be safe.

MS. KYOKO: Anything else?

SHONDRA: Oh, yes. Some people admired her so much that they started calling her Moses or General Tubman.

MS. KYOKO: Shondra, that's terrific. Now, all you have to do is write down what you just said to me!

SHONDRA: You mean I should write the way I talk?

MS. KYOKO: Of course! Now let me show you what two of your note cards will look like. I tried to write down just what you said. Then I added a few details that I'll explain. Look at these two cards:

2-505

Conductor

T. started working w/ Abolitionists as soon as free.

Freed about 200 slaves — took them North.

2-505

preparation for military

People amazed how T seemed to be able
to find food and places for the
runaways to stay.

Admired so much that people called
her Moses or General Tubman.

SHONDRA: Why did you do these as two cards? Why not just one? It was all from one book.

MS. KYOKO: You gave me two ideas. Remember, one idea to a card.

SHONDRA: Oh, that's right. There are two ideas here. But what are these other things you have here? There are some numbers in the upper right corner.

MS. KYOKO: The numbers in the upper right corner are a **code** to tell you where this idea came from. Remember numbering your bibliography cards? [*Shondra nods.*] You numbered this encyclopedia article as 2 and the photocopy shows page 505. So the code 2-505 tells you which page in which book you found this idea.

SHONDRA: I like the code. It's quick and easy! And I do know where these words came from—where you wrote "Conductor" on one card and "Preparation for Military" on the other. Those were words on my tentative plan.

MS. KYOKO: You're right! And we call that part of the note card a **slug.** It's like a label that tells you what this note card has on it.

JUAN: Okay, why a slug? Why does something as short as a note need a label?

MS. KYOKO: Because later, when you're ready to do your report, you will have to organize your note cards. The labels let you organize fast. You'll just put all the note cards together that have the same label. And that's it! You're done!

JUAN: Are you saying that all of our note cards will have these same three parts—the code, the slug, and the note? That's it?

MS. KYOKO: Yes, Juan. Now that's not so hard, is it?

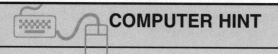

COMPUTER HINT

You can take notes at the keyboard. Before you start though, make sure you can use the equipment for your entire project.

Your hardware and software determine how you can work.

For instance, if you have a single floppy disk drive, take notes and save them in a file. Group notes by slugs, using either the "move" command or by entering text at the right spot. Save the file, and print a copy of your now-organized notes.

Or, if you have a hard disk drive and the right software, take notes, grouped by slugs, and save the file. Later you can call up parts of the file to merge notes into the text file as you need them. For safety, however, be sure to print a copy of your notes.

Always make backup files.

JARROD: The only hard part is what you and Shondra just did. You know—getting the ideas into my own words. I just know I'm going to have trouble with that.

MS. KYOKO: Try doing what Shondra just did. Read the material. Close the book. Then tell somebody about what you've just read. Or if no one is around, talk into a tape recorder. Then write your own words from the tape.

JARROD: Hey, that might work. We can use the tape recorders in the media center.

MS. KYOKO: Good idea.

JUAN: I understand what you and Shondra have been doing. But isn't there ever a time when I would copy somebody else's words onto a note card?

MS. KYOKO: Yes, there are some times when you will want to do that, but not often. Remember, a research report is not a string of quotations you've copied out of your sources.

> ## A research report is not a string of quotations.

Let's say, though, that you find a really powerful passage. Maybe it's just a few words. Maybe it's a sentence or two. You want your audience to hear the exact words. Is that what you're talking about, Juan?

JUAN: I think so.

MS. KYOKO: In that case you may want to copy word for word onto your note cards. If you do, though, you have to be very careful to copy the words just as they are written. And you have to be very careful to use quotation marks around those words to show it's a **direct quotation.**

SHONDRA: You're really stressing this word-for-word and quotation marks bit, Ms. K. Why is that such a big deal?

MS. KYOKO: It's all about something called **plagiarism.**

SHONDRA: Yeow, another big fancy word. Sounds like a contagious disease.

MS. KYOKO: [*Laughing.*] Well, Shondra, it's almost as bad as that. Plagiarism is literary theft. It refers to stealing somebody else's words and using them as your own. But it's simple to avoid the "crime." Do two things: First, put quotation marks around the words. Second, tell your reader who said them.

JUAN: Like Shondra said, you make plagiarism sound pretty bad. Is it really that serious? I mean, I can see how somebody might just forget the quotation marks. You know, like it's not intentional, just careless.

SHONDRA: [*Laughing.*] You mean like Jarrod—just careless! Sorry, Jarr, just teasing.

JARROD: Thanks, but you've got my number. As much as I hate to admit it.

MS. KYOKO: Well, all joking aside, carelessness can be the root of plagiarism.

JARROD: Somebody in my brother Jason's class last year got a really bad grade because she plagiarized. She said she just left out some quotation marks. Jason said she didn't use any quotation marks. Anywhere. He was pretty sure a lot of the paper wasn't in her words. Said it sounded like an encyclopedia.

MS. KYOKO: The problem is, there's no way for your audience to know whether you're sloppy or dishonest. As a result, most people take the "crime" rather seriously. College students have failed classes or even been expelled over it. Government officials have been fired over it. Lawyers have been disbarred for it.

JARROD: Seems to me the message is pretty clear. Don't be careless!

MS. KYOKO: That's it!

SHONDRA: I hate to keep picking at this, but what if we just happened to have four or five words in a row just like some book?

MS. KYOKO: There's a problem only when those four or five words are key phrases. Let's look at some examples. That should help. Here are four paragraphs.

The **first paragraph** is the original passage written by Aurelia Kamp.

The **second paragraph** shows plagiarism.

The **third paragraph** is okay. The original ideas are mostly reworded. A few words are quoted from the original and have quotation marks around them. Finally, a note tells where the quotation comes from.

The **fourth paragraph** is also okay. It's all reworded, and the note at the end tells where the ideas come from.

So here we go with the first two paragraphs.

Paragraph One: Original Passage

The cost-effective production of white corn is important to anyone who likes cereal for breakfast, tacos for lunch, tortillas for dinner, or fritos for a snack. But reducing operating costs in order to keep down consumer costs is an ongoing problem for farmers. As we walked through the grain-bin area, Mr. Z. pointed to a 3,500-gallon propane tank. During the harvest, he explained, the tank was filled every other day. Then, to reduce costs, Mr. Z. spent $70,000 to design and build a cob burner that gasifies the corn cobs and turns them into fuel. The operation has cut the fuel bill by 60%. Now the propane fuel tank is filled only once a week.

Paragraph Two: Plagiarized (Wrong)

Reducing the operating costs of white corn production is an ongoing problem, but one farmer has reduced costs by spending $70,000 to design and build a cob burner that gasifies the corn cobs and turns them into fuel.

SHONDRA: Well, there's no question about literary theft here.

JARROD: Even I can see that.

MS. KYOKO: Good! Notice that some of these words are in a slightly different order from the original. Some words are left out. The paragraph, though, is basically the same. No quotation marks set off Kamp's words. No note tells readers where the words come from. This is totally unacceptable.

Now look at the third paragraph. It's correct. It includes a note that tells the reader the information came from an article by Kamp on page 16.

Paragraph Three: Reworded, Partly Quoted, Documented (Correct)

Farmers try hard to reduce the cost of producing white corn, a staple for many Americans who like cereal and tortillas. One farmer has cut his fuel use in half by using what had once been thrown away: the corn cobs. As Mr. Z. explained, the $70,000 cob burner "gasifies the corn cobs and turns them into fuel" (Kamp 16).

SHONDRA: I can see the difference. Now the only words taken exactly from the first paragraph are in quotation marks. The rest has been reworded the way you showed me earlier.

MS. KYOKO: Good for you, Shondra. Now compare the third paragraph with this fourth one. See if anybody can tell me the difference between them.

Paragraph Four: Reworded and Documented (Correct)

Typical of creative ways to cut the cost of growing white corn, one farmer has given recycling a new twist. For $70,000 he designed and built a cob burner that turns corn cobs to gas. The gas in turn is used for fuel. He is rid of the cobs that piled up out back. At the same time he has cut his fuel use by more than half (Kamp 16).

JARROD: Hey, even I see the difference! This last paragraph summarizes all the ideas of the first one, but the writer uses altogether different words.

JUAN: And even though the stuff is all in the writer's own words, he gives Kamp credit for the ideas.

SHONDRA: This is the kind of note we should write, isn't it, Ms. K.?

MS. KYOKO: Yes. Use paragraphs three and four as your models. Keep them in mind as you take notes. Now, let's summarize. Here's what you do to avoid plagiarism.

HOW TO AVOID PLAGIARISM

1. If you use someone else's words, put them inside quotation marks. Tell who said the words.
2. If you put someone else's words in your own words, tell who said the words.
3. If you summarize someone else's words, tell who gave you the idea.

JUAN: So when we take notes, we should summarize. If we use someone else's words, we put them in quotation marks. Is that it?

MS. KYOKO: That's it! And keep track of where your ideas came from. Use the code for the source, and use the page numbers.

SHONDRA: One other little detail. How do I know when I should use someone else's **exact words?**

MS. KYOKO: Good question. There are two times when using someone else's words makes sense. First, use their exact words when someone who really matters says something about your "little" topic. For instance, maybe the president of the NAACP makes a big statement about Harriet Tubman.

SHONDRA: Okay, maybe this is like what you're talking about. I was skimming this book last night. It talks about

John Brown. He's the guy who tried to free slaves with all these military attacks. You know, the Harpers Ferry raid, when he was caught and hanged. Now we sing that song about John Brown's body lies a'mouldering in the grave. So he really matters, right?

MS. KYOKO: Yes.

SHONDRA: Okay. He said that Harriet Tubman was—and these are his words—"a better officer than most." You know, that supports one idea in my tentative plan. The one about military life.

MS. KYOKO: That's a perfect example of when to use someone else's exact words. Now, Shondra, can you put that on a note card that tells who said those words?

SHONDRA: Sure. [*Writing.*] Like this:

> 9-120
>
> Military life
>
> H. T., according to John Brown (Harpers Ferry) was "a better officer than most."

MS. KYOKO: No problem here! I like the way you use the H.T. abbreviation instead of spelling out her name. Saves time. You've used the quotation marks. And the code in the corner tells you where to give credit for who said the words. The number *9* for the source and the *120* for the page number. Good job.

JARROD: You said there were two times when using someone else's exact words make sense. What's the second?

MS. KYOKO: Ah, yes, the second reason. Sometimes the words
are so tight, so compact, so good that they are really powerful. For instance, we often remember President Kennedy's
words from his inaugural address: "Ask not what your country can do for you, ask what you can do for your country."
That's powerful, tight, concise.

JARROD: I read something like that last night. Jack London
is one of my favorite short story writers. Just so happens he
wrote about the gold rushers. He said, "Their hearts turned
to stone—those which did not break—and they became
beasts."

MS. KYOKO: Good example. Now, can you put that in a note
card?

JARROD: Sure. But don't I need to put in some other things,
like what he was talking about?

MS. KYOKO: Yes, and remember, you don't always have to
write sentences on note cards. Sometimes you can have just
phrases or lists.

JARROD: So [*writing*] how does this look?

3-187

White Pass

Jack London writing about W.P., also
called Dead Horse Trail: "Their hearts
turned to stone — those which did not
break — and they became beasts — the
men on the Dead Horse Trail."

MS. KYOKO: Looks great, Jarrod. Now, let me give you a few hints about two punctuation marks that are special for quoted material.

SHONDRA: Uh-oh. You mean we have to learn more rules for mechanics?

MS. KYOKO: Just two. And you may not need either one. This is just in case! One rule has to do with something called the **ellipsis.** It's a series of three periods separated by a space between each (like this . . .).

JUAN: I've seen that in books. What does it mean?

MS. KYOKO: The ellipsis shows that a word or words have been left out of a quotation. Here's an example.

Original text

But reducing operating costs in order to keep down consumer costs is an ongoing problem for farmers.

Ellipsis used

"But reducing operating costs . . . is an ongoing problem."

JARROD: What happens if I leave words out at the end of a sentence? I'll already have one period there.

MS. KYOKO: Good point. If you leave out words at the end of a sentence and another quoted sentence follows, use four periods. The fourth period is for the end of the sentence.

JUAN: The ellipsis seems easy enough. What's the second punctuation mark?

MS. KYOKO: The other mark is **brackets** [like this]. They are used two ways. You use them to put your own words inside a quotation. Or you use them to change the word form, for example, from *usual* to *usual[ly]*. Look at this example:

127

Original text

The cost-effective production of white corn is important to anyone who likes cereal for breakfast, tacos for lunch, tortillas for dinner, or fritos for a snack.

Brackets used to show own words added

"The cost-effective production of white corn is important to anyone who likes cereal for breakfast, . . . [or] tortillas for dinner . . . ."

MS. KYOKO: The first ellipsis shows I left out the words "tacos for lunch." The second ellipsis shows that "fritos for a snack" is missing and that the sentence ends. Then, to make the sentence read smoothly, I added "or," so it's in brackets. I don't want to make a big deal of these. You may need them, though.

JUAN: Seems simple enough.

MS. KYOKO: At this point, then, let's summarize what kinds of note cards you might be writing.

KINDS OF NOTE CARDS

1. Most note cards will be in your own words.

2. Some may be in someone else's words. These words must be in quotation marks.

3. Some may be a combination of your words and someone else's words.

4. Some note cards may be lists.

5. Some may be all complete sentences.

6. Some may have a mix of phrases and complete sentences.

JARROD: In any case, each will have the same three parts. The code, the slug, and the note. Right?

MS. KYOKO: Exactly! You have that down pat, Jarrod! Now, before you get started, let me warn you of a couple of other possible pitfalls.

JUAN: Uh-oh. I knew this would get complicated. Goodbye to the little three-part note card.

MS. KYOKO: No, Juan, nothing is going to change about the code, the slug, or the note. But as you take notes, you may want to change your tentative plan.

JARROD: Why would I want to change my plan?

MS. KYOKO: Let's say that as you read, you run into some ideas you hadn't thought about. You'll remember we said that the tentative plan is just that—tentative. You can change it. In fact, I'd be surprised if you don't make changes. Some of you will make more changes than others.

CRITICAL THINKING HINT

Your tentative plan guides your note taking. If you are about to take a note for which there is no slug from your plan, you have one of two problems.

1. Your plan needs to change to include the new idea. So revise and use the new slug.

OR

2. The note, while interesting, is not really part of your topic. Don't take notes if they don't help answer your guiding question.

SHONDRA: I think my tentative plan is probably too long. Is it possible that we'll drop some things from our tentative plans?

MS. KYOKO: Of course. In fact, sometimes you have to drop ideas because you don't find any sources that explain them. Before you drop anything, though, ask yourself if you can answer your guiding question without it. Maybe you just have to dig harder to find sources.

SHONDRA: Seems to me we have lots to think about while we're taking notes. Right?

MS. KYOKO: Actually, before you take any note, you should ask yourself three questions: What is this information really telling me? Will this note help answer my guiding question? How can I use this in my project?

THREE QUESTIONS TO ASK YOURSELF BEFORE TAKING ANY NOTE

1. What is this author really saying?
2. How will this information help me answer my guiding question?
3. How can I use this in my research report?

JARROD: Another question. Can we add ideas to our tentative plan as well as drop them?

MS. KYOKO: Sure. Just keep in mind your guiding question. If you want to add an idea, ask yourself if the new idea relates to your guiding question.

JARROD: Can you give me an example to explain that?

MS. KYOKO: Sure. For instance, Jarrod, you may find something about yet another trail into the Klondike. A trail you hadn't considered. Ask yourself if you need to talk about another trail in order to answer your guiding question.

JARROD: That's a good example. My guiding question is "What problems did the gold seekers face on each of the trails to the Klondike?" So don't I have to talk about all the trails?

MS. KYOKO: Well, I don't know, Jarrod. How many trails were there?

JARROD: I don't know yet.

MS. KYOKO: Okay, but you'll know soon enough. Let's think about what you may find. Maybe you'll find there are only two or three trails. Then you can focus on them. On the other hand, if you find out there are eight or ten trails, you'll have to narrow your focus. Maybe you'll do your report on the key problems instead of the key trails.

JARROD: So I may have to reword my guiding question?

MS. KYOKO: Exactly. Just guessing, how do you think you could change it?

JARROD: Could I say, "What problems did the gold seekers face on the main trails into the Klondike?"

MS. KYOKO: You're getting closer! Just keep in mind that many of your early ideas will change as you read and learn about your topic. Always remember:

> **Don't spend more time copying than thinking.**

JUAN: One last question. Do we need to take notes from all our sources?

MS. KYOKO: It's possible that some of your sources will turn

131

out to be useless. But you need to read from a wide variety of sources. In other words, don't end up taking all your notes from one book or one periodical. And be sure you check enough sources.

CRITICAL THINKING HINT

A research project depends on the ideas you find in your sources. You should have about the same number of note cards from each of your main sources.

If you don't have at least a half dozen main sources, you haven't read widely enough.

JARROD: This note taking is going to be a big job.

MS. KYOKO: Granted, it's the biggest of the little jobs. As you read and take notes, you'll find new ideas. You'll find ways to answer your guiding question. The tentative plan will fill out. And finally, you'll have a research report finished!

Remember that writing is a process of discovery!

TIME MANAGEMENT GUIDELINES

Taking notes demands the largest block of time in the research process. You have at least two—and possibly three—jobs going on at the same time.

1. You will read and take notes.
2. You will change your tentative plan as you learn more about your "little" topic.
3. You may have to go back to the library to find other sources.

You will need to discipline yourself to finish on time. Try to work in time blocks of at least an hour without a break. Do some work every day. You need time to read, to take notes, to think, to change your tentative plan, and to find more or different sources. This is not a job you can put off until the last minute.

If your report is due in . . . finish your note taking in . . .

4 weeks	4 days
6 weeks	7 days
8 weeks	9 days
10 weeks	11 days

THREE STUDENTS' PROGRESS

Before you begin your own note taking, listen to Shondra, Juan, and Jarrod talk about their experiences.

SHONDRA: This was a little job that was not so little. I had all these books and magazines piled around me—on the floor, on the table, on my bed, in my book bag. I needed every spare minute to get the job done. I skipped my favorite TV shows all week and—even harder—stayed off the telephone. It's a good thing all my friends are working on their research reports, too. We could all understand each other's problems.

I really had to work to get things into my own words. I tried what Ms. K. suggested. I read, then closed the book, and talked myself through the notes. I had 48 note cards when I finished. Probably only ten had somebody else's words with quotation marks. Everything else was in my own words. But I'm not saying it was any piece of cake.

The big deal was how I changed my tentative plan. And, I mean, I changed it a whole lot. I had my guiding question: "What makes Harriet Tubman such a great woman?" All of a sudden, it was like "Bingo!" One writer kept talking about her military mind. Hey, that made sense! Something clicked. You know, everything that made her special had to do with how she thought. How her mind worked. Here's this tiny little black woman who thinks like a military general.

Then I started wondering. What makes a military mind? I thought about what I was reading. Finally, I came up with three words: disciplined, creative, and bold. These seemed to be the words that earned her so much respect. I started a web with those three words.

My tentative list looked like this:

escaped slavery
parents/family friends/neighbors rescued
conductor of Underground Railroad
no education?
preparation for military?
military life later
clever actions
worked with abolitionists

Now my web looks like this:

Shondra's Concept Web

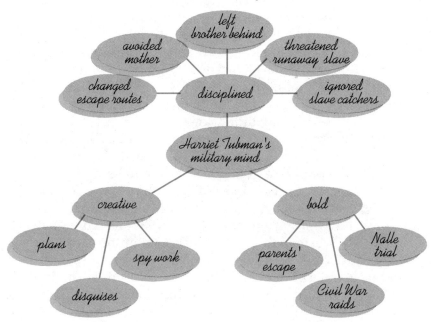

JUAN: Taking notes wasn't as hard for me as for Shondra. Since I'd watched the hawks often at my grandfather's ranch, I knew just a little about them. And since Mr. Mac insists that we write about the animal's life cycle, I knew what was and wasn't worth taking notes on. Because I'm a computer nut, I took all my notes at the keyboard. That's how I work best. Roughly, I'd say I have about 40 note cards.

The best source I had was a book about a family that had a red-tailed hawk as a pet. I ended up reading the whole book. This couple named Wallig kept the hawk until it was strong enough to hunt on its own. Then they released it. Boy, this book told some really neat things about hawks. In fact, I was tempted to take all my notes from this one book, but then I remembered what Ms. K. said: We need lots of sources.

I tried a little strategy that worked for me. Maybe it will help some of you. As soon as I figured out the Wallig book was so good, I forced myself to search through the other books first. Then what information I didn't find in the others, I could get from Wallig. All in all, I found good information in about eight other books.

Then came a little problem. I'd read everything I could find. Still, I had some ideas in my tentative plan that weren't covered. So I called and set up an interview with Mr. Desmond. He's a wildlife biologist who knows about red-tailed hawks. Before the interview, I made a list of questions. For instance, I didn't know whether a hawk catches a mouse with its feet or its beak. I didn't know if they're territorial. I'd read about their courtship flights, but I didn't know if they mate in the air. Stuff like that I still needed to find out.

The interview went great. Mr. Desmond said he liked the fact that I read first and asked questions later. Having the list of questions was really important, too. Without that list, I would have forgotten half the stuff I wanted to ask. Of course, Mr. Desmond's answers are now on my note cards.

The interview really helped fill in the gaps. In fact, just talking about the hawks helped me tune in to some ideas my report should stress. Even if you don't do an interview, you may want to talk about your topic to anyone who will listen—even if it's the family dog. Seems like talking—putting ideas into words you can hear—helps me focus.

JARROD: I had the opposite problem. Taking notes nearly put me under. What with soccer practice and other homework, I had to grab every minute to get my note cards done. Two days I even took notes during lunch. What a drag.

Now, though, I think I have too much information. After I finally figured out there were only three important trails into the Klondike, I used the indexes. Just looked up the three names: Ashcroft, White, and Chilkoot. That really cut down on the reading! Still, sometimes I'd find a whole chapter on one trail—especially the Chilkoot. My guiding question really helped. I kept asking myself, "What experiences did these people have? What kinds of problems did they face? How were the three trails different?" I kept taking notes until I finished going through all my resources. I ended up with about sixty note cards. Whew! It's all so interesting, but I don't know how I'm going to use it all.

And I want to tell you! There are some really gross tales. I guess it was a deadly business—getting there, I mean.

One thing did come of the note taking, though. I have a

better idea of the form for my report. I think I want to do four letters. Three letters—one from a traveler of each trail—will go to one person. Maybe I'll name him Sam, after my uncle. Anyhow, the fourth letter will be Sam's answer, telling which trail he's decided to follow. See, it's pretty clear that the Chilkoot Trail was the most popular—and why. And there's so much about the Chilkoot. The fourth letter would let me talk about all that.

You know, now that I think about it, it sounds like we all changed something after taking notes. Shondra has a whole new plan. Juan added an interview. I have a better idea of form. Ms. Gant says writing is a process of discovery. I guess it really was. For all of us!

JUAN: You bet! Like you, I'm thinking about changing my format. Since I'm such a computer nut, I'd really like to do a computer report—something more than word processing. I'm thinking about a hypermedia report. I'm just thinking. I'll have to see what Mr. Mac says about that.

TIPS AND TRAPS

To share his experiences from last year, here's Jarrod's brother, Jason. He shares hints and warns you of problems you may face taking notes.

JASON: Thanks for asking! So I'll get right down to the nitty-gritty. Three traps and a tip.

First, be sure to use the number code on every note card. I forgot to put the code on a couple of note cards last year. Then I couldn't use the notes because I didn't know where they'd come from. Good information, too. But I didn't have time to root through all those books again to try to find out where the stuff came from. What a downer that was.

Second, don't plagiarize. Check every note card before you put it aside. Check it against whatever you're reading. Don't be sloppy about using someone else's words. It's a bummer to get a really bad grade—or even fail—because of sloppiness.

Third, use exact words only rarely. I know it always
sounds so good in the book. After all, they're professional
writers. But you need to put everything—at least almost
everything—in your own words. Believe me, your report will
be easier to do if you get the note cards into your own
words

Finally, a hint. ***Set a daily goal for yourself.*** This note-
taking business is a really important part of research. You
need to do it well. If you wait until the last minute, you're
doomed. So figure it out. If you have eight days to finish
note cards and eight books to search, then it's obvious. Do
a book a day. I can't beat you over the head and make you
do it. But you'll be beating yourself over the head if you
don't.

Discipline. That's what it takes. Self-discipline.

CHECKLIST

You should be able to answer "yes" to each of these questions.

1. Did I put only one idea on a note card?
2. Did I write on only one side of the card?
3. Did I write in ink?
4. Does every note card include a number code?
5. Does every note card include a slug?
6. Did I avoid using somebody else's words too often?
7. Did I use quotation marks to set off somebody else's words?
8. Did I use brackets, ellipses, and other punctuation marks correctly?
9. Did I avoid plagiarism?
10. Did I avoid taking too many notes from one source?
11. Did I take notes from a wide variety of sources?
12. Do my notes answer my guiding question?
13. Did I change my tentative plan as needed?
14. Did I take enough notes to complete my report?

EXERCISES

Exercise A: Writing a Note in Someone Else's Words

Directions: One student is doing her report on prehistoric mound builders. She wondered why these Native Americans built the mounds. In the passage below find details about mound builders. Then write two notes for her using the author's exact words. Put quotation marks around exact words.

Passage

Indians have roamed the Midwest for over 10,000 years. Archaeologists have divided the 10,000 years into four so-called "traditions": Paleo-Indian, Archaic, Woodland, and Mississippian. Little is known about the Paleo-Indians except that they lived during the last years of the Ice Age. Presumably, they hunted some of the now-extinct animals of the period like wooly mammoths and sabre-toothed tigers.

The Archaic tradition, from about 8000 B.C. until about 1000 B.C., showed change in both the environment and the people's behavior. Archaic Indians hunted and gathered. In later years, they moved their camps only by seasons.

The Woodland tradition dated from roughly 1000 B.C. to A.D. 900. Pottery appeared. Some crop cultivation appeared. Specialized rituals, including elaborate burial rituals and burial mounds, appeared.

Next came the Mississippian tradition, from A.D. 900 to A.D. 1600. They built permanent communities, cultivated crops, and raised a dependable and storable food source—notably maize (or corn), beans, and squash. Another part of the Mississippian tradition was flat-surfaced mounds. These mounds were not for burial as in the Woodland tradition. Instead, their mounds gave a place of honor for important political, social, and religious buildings.

Exercise B: Writing a Combination Note

Directions: Another student is doing his report on the Woodland culture. Review the chart on page 128. Find the information about the Woodland culture in the passage in Exercise A. Write a note that combines your words and the author's words. Make sure the note is appropriate for this student's paper.

Exercise C: Writing in Your Own Words

Directions: A third student is doing her report on the Mississippian traditions. Find the material about the Mississippians in the passage in Exercise A. Make two note cards (one idea to each card) that puts the ideas in your own words. Avoid plagiarism.

Exercise D: Now You Write

Directions: Choose several sources from which you can take a total of five note cards. Take a variety of kinds of notes. Be careful not to plagiarize.

1. Take one note entirely in your own words. Use complete sentences.
2. Take one note entirely in your own words. Use lists or phrases.
3. Take one note with someone else's exact words.
4. Take one note that combines your own words with someone else's exact words.
5. Take one note of your choice.

PEER EDITOR GUIDELINES

When you have finished Exercise D above, take your book, magazine, or other print source along with your note cards to a peer editor. Ask him or her to check for plagiarism. Then have your peer editor use the Checklist on page 138 to check other details on your note cards. Together, make any changes needed.

PORTFOLIO POINTERS

When you and your peer editor have finished checking note cards, answer the following questions. Put your answers in your portfolio.

1. What did I learn from taking these five notes?
2. What did I learn from my peer editor about taking notes?
3. How can I apply what I learned to taking the rest of my notes?

Chapter 7

Getting Organized

You have read the books and magazines. You have read the pamphlets. You have searched for facts, details, and examples. In short, you have gathered all the information you can find. At this point, you should have everything you need to do your report. Now it is time to get organized.

SHONDRA: Whew! That note-taking business was no easy little job, Ms. K. It was one tough job! Please tell us the worst is over.

MS. KYOKO: The worst *is* over. And I'm not just telling you that! We're going to do a series of quick little jobs now that will lead to the first draft of your report.

JUAN: I guess we're all a little suspicious. What do you mean by "quick little jobs"? Little killers?

MS. KYOKO: [*Laughing.*] No, Juan. Let me explain. You have a series of five little jobs. We'll do them one at a time. Here's what we'll do.

1. Check your guiding question.
2. Check your revised plan.

3. Write a thesis sentence.
4. Organize your note cards.
5. Finalize the form.

That doesn't sound so bad, does it?

JUAN: You always make it sound easy.

MS. KYOKO: I promise. This *is* easy. So let's get going. First, we'll start with your **guiding question.** Let's look at yours, Shondra. Did you change your guiding question?

SHONDRA: Well, I started with "What made Harriet Tubman such a great woman?" I ended up with "What character traits show Harriet Tubman's military mind?"

MS. KYOKO: And can you answer that question now?

SHONDRA: I think so. I did the concept web you taught us. By the way, Mr. Koz liked the web. As he said, it helped pinpoint Tubman's three main traits. She was disciplined, creative, and bold. I think these are the traits that show how she thinks.

MS. KYOKO: And can you give examples of each of those traits?

SHONDRA: Yes. They're all in my note cards.

MS. KYOKO: Good, you're all set. What about you, Juan?

JUAN: My guiding question didn't change. It's still "What is a red-tailed hawk's life like?"

MS. KYOKO: Can you answer it now?

JUAN: Yes! With my notes from books and from my interview with Mr. Desmond, I'm set. The hard part for me is thinking of a way to begin my report. I want to talk about the hawk's life without starting out with some dumb thing like "I was born . . ." I still want to impress Mr. Mac with something different.

MS. KYOKO: We'll come back to that, Juan. What about you, Jarrod. Did your guiding question change?

JARROD: Not much. I started out with the guiding question "What problems did gold rushers face on each of the trails?" As you know, I finally took notes on just three trails. So, basically, my question didn't change.

MS. KYOKO: Okay, can you answer the question?

JARROD: I have answers to the question, but they're not the same answers I was looking for. I thought I would find out about how they survived. You know, like what they ate, how they kept warm, if they were ever depressed. I didn't really find that. But I found a ton of other stuff. Even Ms. Gant was impressed.

MS. KYOKO: By "other stuff" do you mean other problems?

JARROD: Yes. Boy, did those guys ever face problems!

MS. KYOKO: Okay, everybody. Check off little job number one! Next. Let's see what changes you made to your **tentative plan.** Shondra, you're using the concept web for your plan, right?

SHONDRA: I'd like to if that's okay. [See Shondra's concept web on page 135.]

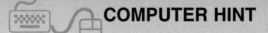

COMPUTER HINT

Some writing programs offer other prewriting tools similar to Shondra's concept web. If you need an outline, some programs will help you make one. Explore the ways these tools will help you finalize your plan.

MS. KYOKO: Of course you may use your concept web. It works just like a list or even an **outline.** Let me show you what I mean. Based on your web, we can write an outline. First, though, tell me something. You have these three key ideas—"disciplined," "creative," and "bold." Which one do you want to write about first?

SHONDRA: I have no idea. Does it make any difference?

MS. KYOKO: Every plan needs some logic to it. You can use four ways to put logic into your plan. Maybe the logic is **time.** What happens first in a hawk's life? What's next? Or maybe the logic is **space.** What did the gold seekers face as they moved south to north? Sometimes the logic is **order of importance.** What was the least important trait of Tubman's military mind? The most important? Sometimes the logical plan is a **combination** of these.

CRITICAL THINKING HINT

Use one of the following ways of ordering information to plan your report:

1. Time Order

Time order follows the calendar or the clock. The pattern moves from yesterday, to today, to tomorrow. A research report that tells about a historical event, for instance, may be in time order.

2. Space Order

Space order follows a pattern in distance. You can organize from near to far, far to near, left to right, right to left, front to back, back to front, top to bottom, or bottom to top. A description of a battlefield, for instance, may be in space order from the viewer's left to right.

3. Orders of Importance

There are three orders of importance.

from least important to most
from most important to least
from second most important to least important to
most important

This last plan lets you start with something important enough to keep your reader's attention and still end with a wallop—the most important. A political campaign speech, for instance, may be in an order of importance. It will probably end with the most important reason to vote for the candidate.

4. Combinations

A research report may combine orders of importance with time order. It could also combine time order with space order, space order with an order of importance, or a combination of all three ways of ordering.

For instance, a chart about rain forests may follow time order to show how the forests have disappeared. A map would use space order to explain where rain forests remain around the world. A written part may follow an order of importance to explain the reasons for saving rain forests.

SHONDRA: Let me think a minute. The examples I have about "disciplined" come from Tubman's early years. The Underground Railroad and all. The "creative" part comes afterward. In fact, two of the three examples for "bold" come afterward, too.

MS. KYOKO: So what do you think that tells you?

SHONDRA: If I use time order, I guess I'd do "disciplined," then "creative," and then "bold."

JUAN: That's really a kind of order of importance, too, Shondra. It's like she got stronger, militarily at least.

SHONDRA: Good point, Juan. That's true, now that I think about it.

MS. KYOKO: Okay, then, let me put your web into an outline, just to illustrate.

    I. Disciplined
       A. Left brother behind
       B. Avoided mother
       C. Changed escape routes
       D. Threatened Underground Railroad passengers
       E. Ignored slave catchers

    II. Creative
       A. Planned escapes
       B. Used disguises
       C. Spied on Rebels

    III. Bold
       A. Parents' escape
       B. Nalle trial
       C. Civil War raids

If your teacher wants a formal outline with your report, use the following chart as a guide to develop your own. Use the model above to check details like spacing, indentation, punctuation, and capitalization.

WRITING AN OUTLINE

If your report must have a formal outline, use Shondra's as a model. To write your own, follow these easy steps:

1. Start with your guiding question. From your tentative plan or concept web, find the three or four ideas that answer the question. These are your main ideas.

2. Put the main ideas in a logical order (by time, space, importance, or a combination). Mark the order with Roman numerals: I, II, III, IV.

3. Study the remaining ideas in your tentative plan or web. Group them under the main ideas they explain. These are your supporting ideas.

4. Put each group of supporting ideas in a logical order. Note the order with capital letters: A, B, C, etc.

TWO HINTS:

1. Make sure you use only words or phrases in your outline. Do not use sentences unless your teacher asks you to.

2. Be sure to use similar kinds of words for each part of your outline. This is called parallelism. For instance, all of Shondra's main ideas are adjectives. All of the supporting ideas in parts I and II are verbs with direct objects. All of the supporting ideas in part III are adjectives with nouns.

SHONDRA: So the only difference between my web and an outline is some letters and numbers. That's a snap!

CRITICAL THINKING HINT

Here are two suggestions that might prove helpful:

First, if you have trouble making your final plan, put your note cards aside. Tell a peer what you've learned about your topic. By talking, you will find the main ideas more easily.

Second, the form of your plan is not as important as its logic. Think about the two or three main ideas you want to share with your audience. Then think about ways to explain those two or three ideas. Whether you write an outline or draw a "picture" of your plan (like Shondra's web) doesn't matter.

MS. KYOKO: I'm glad you see how easy this is, Shondra. I don't care how you organize. You can use a web, a map, an outline, or any other graphic organizer. Just so you have a plan. So Juan, what does your plan look like?

JUAN: Not much. In fact, I don't really have a plan. I don't think I need one. I'm just telling a story. You know, writing as if I'm the hawk.

MS. KYOKO: You mean, writing in first person.

JUAN: Yes, I think the paper will be more interesting that way. After all, Mr. Mac is going to be reading a bunch of these reports. I want mine to be a little different. Maybe I'll get a better grade that way.

MS. KYOKO: You're probably right about that. But you still need a plan.

> Every report needs a plan.

Whether it's an audio tape, a skit, a letter file, a portfolio, a newspaper, or a musical score, you need a plan. The plans may look different. In fact, if you have several forms to your report, for example, a letter, an audio tape, and a map— you need two plans. An overall plan and a plan for each part.

JUAN: I just have to get the hawk from birth to death. He— or she—has to reach maturity, find a mate, raise young, cope with problems, and die. What more is there? Isn't that a plan?

MS. KYOKO: It could be. But you said you didn't want to start with something like "I was born . . ." Why not think about the stories you've read lately? They usually begin with a crisis and go from there. Short stories don't begin with "I was born . . ."

JUAN: Ummm. Yes. Or like a lot of TV shows. They begin with a crisis. Some kind of action. Gets your attention—so you won't flip channels!

MS. KYOKO: That's it exactly. You don't want Mr. McKenney to flip channels on you, either. Why not use a story map to make your plan. You know, your report will probably read more like a short story than like the paper Shondra is doing.

JUAN: Maybe that will help. I'll give it a try.

MS. KYOKO: Okay, Jarrod. What does your revised plan look like?

JARROD: Simple. It just takes in the three trails. I can organize each letter in the order that things happened along the trail. See, each letter is a story of what happened to some imaginary character on the trail.

MS. KYOKO: Can you put that in an outline or graphic organizer?

JARROD: Well, it's a bare-bones outline.

    I. Ashcroft Trail
       A. Beginning
       B. Middle
       C. End
   II. White Pass Trail
       A. Beginning
       B. Middle
       C. End
  III. Chilkoot Trail
       A. Beginning
       B. Middle
       C. End

MS. KYOKO: Did you have a reason for putting the trails in that order?

JARROD: Yes. The Ashcroft was the least popular and the Chilkoot the most popular.

MS. KYOKO: Good for you, Jarrod! Saving the best for last. That's a good organizational plan. Okay, then. Check off little job number two! Next. You need a **thesis sentence.**

JARROD: What's a thesis sentence?

MS. KYOKO: A thesis sentence says what your paper is about. In fact, it's really a combination of your guiding question and your plan.

JUAN: That's confusing. Can you explain that?

MS. KYOKO: Better yet, let's use Shondra's question and outline as an example.

SHONDRA: I'm all for that!

MS. KYOKO: I thought you would be! Now, Shondra, your guiding question was "What character traits show Harriet Tubman's military mind?" Put that question into a statement.

SHONDRA: You mean just turn the question around? [*Ms. K. nods.*] Like this, then: "Certain character traits show Harriet Tubman's military mind."

MS. KYOKO: Good. Now add to that sentence the three main ideas from your concept web.

SHONDRA: I think I understand. Is this it? "Discipline, creativity, and boldness are the character traits that show Harriet Tubman's military mind."

MS. KYOKO: Good. Now can you tighten that sentence?

SHONDRA: I don't understand.

JUAN: Maybe I do. Couldn't she say, "Her discipline, creativity, and boldness show Harriet Tubman's military mind"?

MS. KYOKO: That's one way, Juan. Do you get the idea now, Shondra?

SHONDRA: Sure! So that's my thesis sentence?

MS. KYOKO: Yes!

CRITICAL THINKING HINT

Writing a thesis sentence is like stating the main idea of your report. If you have trouble putting your whole report into one sentence, talk to a peer. Begin with, "The purpose of my report is to . . ." Then fill in the blank.

MS. KYOKO: Juan, what about your thesis sentence?

JUAN: Well, I don't know. It sounds kind of silly to say "The red-tailed hawk is born, faces problems, and dies." Do I have to have a thesis sentence for a first-person narrative? It's going to read like a story.

MS. KYOKO: Yes, Juan. A thesis is part of your plan. Every report needs a plan and a sense of direction. The thesis sentence gives you—and maybe your audience—a sense of direction.

JUAN: I still think the thesis sentence I read sounds silly.

JARROD: I'm glad you said that Juan—it does sound silly. You know, you could say "Following a red-tailed hawk's life helps people understand how the bird fits in the balance of nature."

JUAN: [*gives Jarrod a high five*] That's good! C'mon, Jarr, how did you come up with that?

JARROD: Well, you know that's the kind of stuff science teachers like to hear. That balance-of-nature thing.

JUAN: I guess you're right. You know, Mr. Mac told us whatever animal we chose had to face at least two problems. One has to be natural and the other caused by people. He says that's part of understanding an animal's place in the world.

MS. KYOKO: Are you okay with this thesis, then? Does it say what you plan to do in your first-person narrative?

JUAN: Exactly! It's great. Thanks, Jarr!

MS. KYOKO: [*turns to Jarrod*] Well, hotshot! Do you have a good thesis sentence for yourself?

JARROD: How about "Gold rushers into the Klondike mostly followed one of three trails."

JUAN: Okay, now it's my turn. Maybe it's easier to see somebody else's solutions than your own. At any rate, Jarr, that sentence doesn't do it.

JARROD: I'll take all the help I can get. Tell me what you mean.

JUAN: There's nothing in the sentence about the problems they faced. That's what you're really writing about, isn't it? Their problems?

CRITICAL THINKING HINT

Make sure your thesis sentence has two parts:

Part 1: the subject (for Jarrod, the trails into the Klondike)

Part 2: your view of it (for Jarrod, the problems of taking the trails)

JARROD: Good point. Ummm. How about this? "Gold rushers faced tough problems on each of the three main trails into the Klondike." What do you think, Ms. K.?

MS. KYOKO: Much, much better! Check off little job number three! Next. **Organize the note cards.**

SHONDRA: Let me guess. We sort our note cards so that they are in the same order as our revised plans. Right?

MS. KYOKO: You're right on target. In other words, you'll have your note cards in the order you will need them to do your report—whatever its form.

JARROD: Is there some easy way to sort them? I mean, what do we do—read them all again?

MS. KYOKO: I hope not! That's why you used slugs, so you wouldn't have to read them all. Do the sorting in two steps:

1.   Use the slugs to create a stack of note cards for each major idea.
2.   Put the stacks in order.

CRITICAL THINKING HINT

To put the stacks in order is to arrange them according to your revised plan. As you put the stacks in order, think about what you have.

Do you need to further revise your plan?

Did you forget about some ideas you found?

Do you have some note cards that seem not to fit your plan?

Don't throw away cards that "don't fit." At the same time, don't force then into your plan. You will lose the logic.

[Later]

SHONDRA: Okay, check off little job number four! I think we all have our note cards in order.

MS. KYOKO: Checked! Next. Finalize the **form.** Remember all of you talked about the forms you wanted to use. Who's doing what?

SHONDRA: I'm sticking with the regular paper. I know I need to do that for college, so I might as well learn now.

JUAN: I'm set. The first-person narrative works for me. I may do it on the computer, though. Depends on how much time I have.

JARROD: Here we go again. I'm the one who still isn't sure. I think I'm doing a letter file. You know, four personal letters. But what if it doesn't work? Can we change our minds once we get into the actual writing?

MS. KYOKO: A letter file is fine. But, yes, you can change your mind. Remember you have many choices. You may decide to add some other parts.

JARROD: You mean something in addition to letters?

MS. KYOKO: Sure. In fact, all of you may decide to add something. For instance, Shondra, you may want to add a map to show where Tubman traveled along the Underground Railroad. Juan, you may want to add some pictures. I don't think I've seen a red-tailed hawk. What does its nest look like? Where does it live? Maybe a map could show that.

SHONDRA: So if the form we choose doesn't seem to be working, we can go in a different direction?

MS. KYOKO: Yes. But I doubt that anybody will totally change directions. More likely, you'll make additions. You may find better ways to get certain points across. Go back and review Chapter 2. Remember you had about 90 suggestions for form there!

COMPUTER HINT

You may find a form the computer can help you with. If you are a serious traveler in cyberspace, check the hypermedia programs. They will let you use many media, including quicktime visuals and audio. You can scan photos and maps into the program. With "buttons" you can send your audience vertically or horizontally through your report.

Even if you are only a sometime traveler on the information highway, many programs can help. For instance, you can design brochures, banners, fliers, charts and other visuals at the keyboard. Most of these programs require you to be familiar with their use. Plan ahead.

CRITICAL THINKING HINT

Ask yourself questions as you think about your own form or combination of forms:

1. Is there a form that will help me explain something? A chart? A graph? A map? A picture? An audio tape?

Example: One student reported on his city's architecture. He planned to use pictures with captions and to write about the architects. Before he finished, he mapped a walking tour. The map sent tourists through the area to see the buildings he had photographed. Then, he added an audio tape to talk them through the walking tour.

2. Does my report talk about something that my audience can't see in their mind's eye? It could be a place they've never been, a person they've never met, or an object they've never seen. If so, what visual can I use to help? A poster? A slide? A photograph? A video?

Example: Another student did his report on what visitors see in southern Utah. To help readers understand the land, he used pictures of area national parks. He showed Arches, Capitol Reef, Bryce Canyon, and Zion national parks. Using string, he linked pictures to spots on a Utah map. The pictures and map illustrated his written report.

3. Does my report talk about something my audience needs to hear? A concert? A musician? A speaker? If so, add a tape or recording.

Example: A third student did her report on Kwanzaa, an African-American cultural holiday. Since music is a big part of it, she included an audio tape of music.

MS. KYOKO: Okay. Check off little job number five! The worst is over.

TIME MANAGEMENT GUIDELINES

It should take only a few hours to complete these five little jobs: 1. Check your guiding questions. 2. Check your revised plan. 3. Write a thesis sentence. 4. Organize your note cards. 5. Finalize the form. Allow no more than one day, no matter how long you have to finish your final report.

THREE STUDENTS' PROGRESS

You followed Shondra, Juan, and Jarrod through each of the five little jobs. You heard each talk about a new guiding question, revised plan, and thesis sentence. Finally, each organized his or her note cards and reviewed plans6 for form. Listen to their final words of experience.

SHONDRA: Finally! My note cards are sorted. I had slugs that matched my tentative plan, so I had to figure out which new heading the slugs matched. I'm sure glad each idea is on a different note card. Otherwise I'd never get this stuff in any kind of order. I think what I have now will work. Mr. Koz ought to like this report!

JUAN: My biggest job was getting a plan. After Ms. K. suggested the story map, things started falling in place. I decided to start my story when the hawk is almost mature. Since Mr. Mac says our animals have to face a man-made danger, I'll begin with some kids shooting and wounding the hawk. Of course the hawk survives. Otherwise, I wouldn't have a report! Then, so I can tell about the whole life cycle, I'll talk about his offspring hatching and growing up. Here's the story map I came up with.

Story Map

Title: *My Life: The Red-Tailed Hawk*

Author: *Juan*

Characters: *male red-tailed hawk, female, humans*

Setting: (Time) *begins in early fall: covers 3 years*

(Place) *generic red-tailed hawk territory*

Problem: *survive man-made and natural crises*

Goal: *to live full life cycle*

Events Leading to Resolution of Goal:

Event 1: *shot and wounded by humans*

Event 2: *attacked by fox*

Event 3: *finds food; can fly again*

Event 4: *meets female*

Event 5: *builds nest and raises young*

Final Event/Turning Point: *humans invade territory*

Resolution: *killed by truck*

JARROD: I'm still nervous about all this. I have this thesis sentence, thanks to Juan's help. I have a plan, but it seems too simple. I just don't know what else to write down. The one thing that did work for me was getting the note cards in order. That's because I had good slugs. I think my letter file is still the way to go on form, and Ms. Gant agrees. But I might have to add a map or something. So I have everything Ms. K. says we need to have. I'm just really nervous. Sometimes when I think about it my stomach churns like it does before a big soccer match.

TIPS AND TRAPS

Some students slide over these steps and do not get fully organized. They think they should just begin. Don't be one of them. Get a clear plan. Write a good thesis sentence. Some students write the thesis sentence and then polish the plan. Others polish the plan and then do the thesis. Do whatever works better for you.

Jason, Jarrod's brother, has more advice for Jarrod and his peers.

JASON: It's tempting to just jump in and start writing or start putting your report together. Forget it. It's like going for your driver's license without studying for the test. You have to pass the test or it's no license. You have to get organized or it's no research report. So get those note cards in logical order. Have a reason for putting them in the order you do.

Don't start writing until you know exactly where you're going. Your plan is like a road map. Follow it and you'll reach your destination. Otherwise you'll get lost.

CHECKLIST

You should be able to answer "yes" to the following questions.

1. Is my reworded guiding question clear?
2. Do I have a revised plan in an outline or a graphic organizer?
3. Do I have a clearly worded thesis sentence?
4. Does the thesis sentence say what my research report is really going to do?
5. Have I organized my note cards to follow my revised plan?
6. Have I settled on the form or forms I want to use?

EXERCISES

Exercise A: Choosing a Good Thesis

Directions: A good thesis sentence names the subject and gives the writer's view of it. In these pairs of thesis sentences, one is better than the other. Choose the better sentence. Be able to tell what is missing from the weaker sentence.

1. a. Watching a baseball game on television is better than being there in person.
    b. You can watch baseball games on television, or you can go to the ballpark.
2. a. Everyone should eat three meals a day.
    b. Eating three well-balanced meals a day helps a person's mind, body, and attitude.
3. a. A bird's light body, strong chest muscles, and feathers make it able to fly better than an airplane.
    b. Birds can fly better than airplanes.
4. a. Television is called a great teacher but is also labeled as the cause of poor reading and writing skills.
    b. Television influences almost everyone's daily lives.
5. a. The inside of a Pilgrim house was simple.
    b. A Pilgrim house had few necessities and no luxuries.
6. a. Paul Revere took a midnight ride and also worked as a successful silversmith.
    b. Paul Revere's silverware designs and engravings show great talent.
7. a. Religious and practical reasons determined where pyramids were built.
    b. Pyramids were built on the west bank of the Nile River.
8. a. The nomadic Huns helped cause the fall of Rome.
    b. The end of the Roman Empire came in the third century.
9. a. Mongols live in yurts, which are domed shelters made of fur.
    b. The Mongols' living and eating habits reflect the fact that they move with their animals.

10. a. Desert animals have adapted to their environment by changing their color, their eating habits, and their living habits.
    b. The major deserts in the United States are located between the Rocky Mountains and the Sierra Nevada.

Exercise B: Choosing a Logical Order

Directions: Put the items in these groups in logical order. Name the order (time, space, importance), and be able to tell why you chose the order. More than one order may be logical for each group. The common group is named for you.

1. **Modes of Dress:** suit and tie, shorts and tank top, jeans and polo shirt
2. **Fruits:** cantaloupe, apples, grapes, watermelon
3. **Cities:** New York, Chicago, Miami, Los Angeles
4. **Playing Fields:** basketball, baseball, table tennis, golf
5. **Means of Transportation:** bicycle, airplane, train, automobile, ship
6. **Music Recordings:** compact disk, phonograph record, cassette tape
7. **Weather:** hurricane, thunderstorm, sunshine, spring shower
8. **Wars:** American Revolution, Vietnam War, Civil War, Persian Gulf War
9. **Pets:** dog, bird, snake, spider
10. **States:** Rhode Island, Texas, North Carolina

Exercise C: Thinking about Plans

Directions: Answer these questions about the plans you have seen for Shondra's, Jarrod's, and Juan's research reports.

1. Study Shondra's plan on page 147. Name at least four things that are good about her plan.
2. Study Jarrod's plan on page 151. Why do you think Jarrod is worried about his plan?

162

3. Study Juan's story map on page 159. What do you like best about his plan?

4. Would a story map like Juan's work for Jarrod? Why or why not?

5. Would a plan like Shondra's or Jarrod's work for Juan? Why or why not?

Exercise D: Thinking about Form

Directions: Shondra plans a traditional paper. She could also use many other forms. Pretend you are her reader. Tell what each of these forms could do for her report. (You may need to refer to Chapter 2, pages 31–38, to review the forms and their purposes.) An example is completed for you.

Example: maps—show where Tubman grew up, the route she followed on the Underground Railroad, where the Civil War raids were

1.	letters	9.	newspaper
2.	poster	10.	editorial cartoon
3.	role playing	11.	brochure
4.	interview	12.	résumé
5.	skit	13.	advertisement
6.	audio tape	14.	children's book
7.	video tape	15.	debate
8.	television talk show		

Exercise E: Now You Write

Directions: Write and/or revise the following for your own research report.

1. Clearly worded guiding question
2. Revised plan in the form of an outline or a graphic organizer
3. Clearly worded thesis sentence
4. A sentence explaining how you will use each form chosen for your report

PEER EDITING GUIDELINES

When you have finished Exercise E, ask a peer editor or someone from your writing group to talk with you about your responses. Your peer editor should use the following questions.

1. Does the thesis sentence answer the guiding question? What revisions can I suggest?
2. What is the writer's attitude toward his or her subject? Is it clear?
3. Does the plan do what the thesis sentence says? What revisions can I suggest?
4. Has the writer chosen the best form or forms for his or her report? Why or why not?
5. What other forms should the writer consider? Why?

PORTFOLIO POINTERS

When you and your peer editor finish the questions above, answer the following questions. Then clip together your answers to Exercise E, your peer editor's comments, and the answers to the following questions. Put them in your portfolio.

1. So far, what do I like best about my research report? Why?
2. What has been the most difficult part for me so far? Why?
3. What have I learned about doing a research report?
4. If I had to start another research report tomorrow, what would I do differently? Why?

Chapter 8

Creating the First Draft

The research is done. You have note cards to support each of your main ideas. Your guiding question is now a thesis sentence. Your plan is revised. You have thought more about form. In other words, you are organized. Now you are ready to put everything together. If all has gone well up to now, doing your first draft should be easy.

MS. KYOKO: All right! You're ready to do the first draft. Before you begin, I'll give you some pointers. Since everyone will have to do some writing as part of the report, you can all use some tips. Then we'll get to the nitty-gritty about the various forms.

JARROD: We're all doing such different kinds of reports. How can you help all of us at once?

MS. KYOKO: With some general hints. First, no matter what you're writing, use ink. Sure, you'll make changes, draw arrows, cross things out, add others. But if you use pencil, your work will smear, and you'll probably have erasure holes.

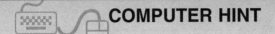

COMPUTER HINT

If you are writing at a word processor, set the page format for double-spaced or even triple-spaced lines. Since you will no doubt revise both on screen and on copy, wide spacing will give more room.

JUAN: I'll probably do mine on the word processor. I'm better at the keyboard than with a pen in hand.

JARROD: Not me. I'm too slow at the keyboard. Good ol' pen and paper for me. But what other hints, Ms. K.?

MS. KYOKO: Second, write on only one side of the paper. And write on every other line. Later, if you need to cut paragraphs and sentences apart and tape them together in a different order, you can do it easily. Writing on every other line leaves space for editing and revising.

JARROD: Good hints, Ms. K. I wish somebody had told me these things years ago. I can use these hints when I write in any of my classes.

MS. KYOKO: Of course, Jarrod. These are things you learn with practice. You know what they say in sports—no pain, no gain! But there's more. Remember never to throw anything away.

SHONDRA: I like to get rid of rubbish. Why shouldn't we throw anything away?

MS. KYOKO: It's tempting to throw away drafts that don't work or note cards that don't fit. Instead, keep a big envelope labeled "trash." Put everything in it you'd otherwise throw away. Without fail, what you throw away today you'll need tomorrow.

JARROD: Hey, I've done that. And I never need anything

that's still in the wastebasket. It's always something I threw away before the trash pick-up day.

MS. KYOKO: One last hint. Stay on track. Follow your plan. Some beginning writers seem to forget why they made a plan. It's to follow!

CRITICAL THINKING HINT

As you write, keep asking yourself this question: Does this detail help me (and my audience) answer my guiding question? If you can't answer "yes," drop it. Stick to your plan!

SHONDRA: This all sounds good. You know what I'm worried about, though? Getting started. When I start to write, that blank page gives me the creeps.

MS. KYOKO: No matter what form you use, you have the same problem—how to begin. Not everyone begins the same way. You may want to begin at the beginning and move right through. You may want to begin with another part of the report and do the beginning last. Do what works for you.

COMPUTER HINT

For a written report, make use of the block command. You can move whole paragraphs or groups of paragraphs to try them in a different order. You may find that something you planned to talk about first, fits better last, or in the middle. If the move doesn't work, it's easy to put text right back where it was.

MS. KYOKO: Let's look at some ideas for your beginning, or **introduction.** Remember the first job of the introduction is to get the reader's or listener's attention. I can help you get started with that.

JARROD: Sounds good to me. But I'm doing a series of letters. Will they have an introduction?

MS. KYOKO: Yes. Remember this little hint:

> **Every report—and every part of a report—has a beginning, a middle, and an end.**

SHONDRA: What do you mean?

MS. KYOKO: Let me give you two examples. Say you're writing the script for an interview. The interview will have a beginning, middle, and end. The beginning gets the listener's attention. Gives some background. The middle is the heart of the interview. That's where the real details come in. The end makes a final comment or summary.

JARROD: My letters are a little like an interview, I guess. But you said two examples. What's the other?

MS. KYOKO: Even a sales brochure has the same three parts. The beginning gets the reader's attention. The middle tells about the product or service—or whatever it's selling. And the end tries to get the reader to act—that is, to buy.

JARROD: My letters have to begin somewhere. I just never thought about planning the beginning.

MS. KYOKO: I understand what you're saying, Jarrod. True, you won't use the same beginning in a letter as you would for an essay that you'd write for Ms. Gant. But you'll need something at the beginning.

CRITICAL THINKING HINT

When you create your beginning, think about how to get audience attention. Will they be interested in your topic? Will they be yawning as soon as they hear it? Will they scratch their heads in confusion?

To make a good beginning, guess at your audience's first thoughts about your topic. Let your beginning do what it must to gain their interest.

JARROD: So, what are some of the ways to begin?

MS. KYOKO: The beginning needs to catch the reader's or listener's **attention.** In general, there are five ways to do that.

WAYS TO CATCH ATTENTION

1. Surprise the audience with facts or numbers.

2. Describe something forceful or shocking.

3. Use a story or conversation.

4. Ask a question.

5. Use a quotation or saying.

JARROD: I'm not sure how to do any of these five. Can you give us some examples?

MS. KYOKO: Sure. Let's start with **surprising the audience**

with facts or numbers. Here's one. Assume a person could count twenty-four hours a day. If he did, it would take 31,688 years to count to a trillion!

SHONDRA: No kidding! That *is* surprising. Where do you find facts like that?

MS. KYOKO: In the library! It could be the beginning for a report on the national debt. Let's go on with our examples. You can **describe something forceful or shocking.** I was reading an article last night about wetlands. [*Hunts for her glasses.*] Here's the way it began:

> Quaking bogs and snake-infested, mosquito-ridden swamps make up the stuff of chiller movies. The gooey slime hides both crime and criminal. The gloom is home to creepy crawly things.

SHONDRA: Yuck. That's disgusting. Oh, I guess you guys probably think that's great.

JUAN: [*Grinning*] Aw, com'on, Shondra. Haven't you ever been in a wetland? It's funny to watch you react that way to one of nature's most awesome places.

SHONDRA: Still sounds yucky to me. So why would an article begin like that?

MS. KYOKO: Because, as you've just proven, that's the way lots of people think of wetlands. The article went on to explain how wrong we are for thinking that way. But it was an attention-getting start!

JARROD: I could do a beginning like that with my letters. I found lots of gory details about the lives of the stampeders. It would definitely be shocking. It may be more than Ms. Gant can take, though.

MS. KYOKO: You have to use good judgment, but it may be work for you, Jarrod. Or, you might use a **story or conversation** to begin. Lots of letters tell stories, you know. A student last year wrote her research report about the changes in Russia. She began this way:

At the bakery, Yvette stood in line for two hours this morning. She wanted a loaf of bread for her three children, her husband, and herself. Just one loaf. When she finally reached the head of the line, a weary clerk told her, "No more bread. Try tomorrow."

JUAN: That's really a good story. It makes us feel sorry for this character, Yvette.

MS. KYOKO: Exactly. A good beginning, or a good introduction, needs to pull the reader or listener into the subject. Another way to do that is to **ask a question.** A report on proper dress might begin with a question like, "What purpose does a man's tie have?" Or "Why would a woman walk on the balls of her feet just to wear high heels?"

SHONDRA: If I use a question to begin, do I answer it somewhere in my report?

MS. KYOKO: Yes! You've hooked your audience. You can't disappoint them!

JUAN: You also said we could start with a quotation or saying. How about an example?

MS. KYOKO: Sure. You can find all kinds of **quotations and adages** in a variety of dictionaries. Most are called dictionaries of thought or dictionaries of quotations. Use the index to find an appropriate quotation for your topic.

JUAN: So if I wanted a quotation for my report, I look up "hawks"?

MS. KYOKO: Maybe. Or maybe "birds." Here's a dictionary of quotations from our library. What do you find under "birds"?

JUAN: [*Hunts entry.*] Two pages of quotations! This one's good: "A Robin redbreast in a cage/ Puts all heaven in a rage." I guess that means to cage any wild bird is wrong. Well, I can certainly agree with that. Should I use it in my paper?

MS. KYOKO: What do you think?

JUAN: I don't know. It doesn't seem to fit what I'm doing. I'm talking about a hawk, not a robin. And it won't be caged.

MS. KYOKO: You're right; it doesn't fit.

SHONDRA: So how do we know how to begin? Which introduction is best?

MS. KYOKO: Introductions are like shoes. You have to try them on and see how they fit.

JARROD: What else do we need to know to do the beginning?

MS. KYOKO: The beginning needs to set the stage for your report. You have to get the readers' attention. Then you have to get them in the right **frame of mind.** Let them know what they're going to be reading about.

SHONDRA: What do you mean by "right frame of mind"?

MS. KYOKO: Let's say you introduce your report on Harriet Tubman with a funny story. You put the audience in a humorous frame of mind. As a result, they assume you're going to write an amusing report. Imagine Mr. Koz thinking he's going to get a humorous report and then disappointing him!

SHONDRA: I see your point. Nobody loves a funny story better than Mr. Koz. But Tubman's story is pretty serious. So if my report isn't funny, I shouldn't start out funny.

MS. KYOKO: Precisely!

CRITICAL THINKING HINT

Never use stories, facts, quotations, startling statements, or other attention-getters for their own sake. Be sure they have a direct link to your purpose. You want your audience to be open-minded about your topic. What will help you get them in the right frame of mind?

JARROD: We get audience attention. Put them in the right frame of mind. And what was that other thing you mentioned?

MS. KYOKO: Let your audience know **what they're going to be reading** or hearing.

JUAN: You mean, we give them the thesis sentence?

MS. KYOKO: That's one way. Certainly in a paper like yours, Shondra. For you, the thesis sentence is part of the introduction. Other forms use other ways to tell the audience about the topic. A map, for instance, has a legend. A cover letter may introduce a letter file. A narrator may introduce an interview or a skit.

SHONDRA: That makes sense. So, the introduction has three purposes: To get audience attention. To put them in the right frame of mind. And to tell them what they'll be hearing or reading about. Is that it?

MS. KYOKO: That's it.

THREE PURPOSES OF THE INTRODUCTION

1. Get the audience's attention.
2. Put them in the right frame of mind.
3. Tell them what they'll be hearing or reading about.

JARROD: After the introduction, then what? What do we need to know about the middle?

MS. KYOKO: The **middle—or body—**of the report follows your plan.

CRITICAL THINKING HINT

To follow your plan is to explain each part of it. For instance, you may be writing a paper. If you're using an outline, write a paragraph for each part of the outline. If you're using a graphic organizer, write a paragraph for each part in the web.

If you are not using a traditional writing form, explain each part of your plan by using a chart, audio tape, letter, skit, and so on.

JUAN: And our note cards give us the details. We use them to explain our main ideas. Is that it?

MS. KYOKO: Exactly. In fact, let's use some note cards to show you how that happens. Shondra, how about a few of your cards? Do you have four or five cards with the same slug?

SHONDRA: Sure. Let's see. [*She looks through her cards.*] Okay, here are four cards that have the same slug—"Nalle Trial."

MS. KYOKO: Good. I remember "Nalle Trial" as a circle on your concept web. Let's see. Was that something about her boldness? Do I remember correctly?

SHONDRA: That's right.

MS. KYOKO: Okay. Let's see what's on the four cards. [*She hunts for her glasses; finds them hanging from a chain around her neck.*]

Nalle trial   9-13

Charles Nalle freed 10 years. Fugitive
Slave Act said had to be returned to
master.

9-14

Nalle trial

Big crowd outside cheering, chanting.

9-15

Nalle trial

H. T. had plan for Nalle to escape. Wagon
waiting. When he made run, she took on
cops. Was "repeatedly beaten over the head
with policemen's clubs, but she never for
a moment released her hold... [and]
suffered their blows without flinching."
Escaped w/ Nalle.

9-15

Nalle trial

H. T.'s actions made headlines next
day.

SHONDRA: That's all I have on the Nalle Trial. Is that enough for a paragraph?

MS. KYOKO: Probably. We'll see. These notes really show a bold woman! You were right to put "Nalle Trial" under the "bold" heading. Feisty little thing, wasn't she!

SHONDRA: You bet!

MS. KYOKO: Okay, let's work together and write a paragraph with these note cards. You've all had Ms. Gant for English, so you know about writing good paragraphs. Let's start with a topic sentence. Can you come up with one?

SHONDRA: Ummm. Well, this is about Tubman's boldness. So the topic sentence should have something about boldness and the trial, right?

MS. KYOKO: Exactly. Any idea? Anybody?

JUAN: How about "Harriet Tubman showed her boldness at the Nalle Trial"?

MS. KYOKO: That's a decent topic sentence. Let's start there. What's next?

JARROD: Well, we put supporting ideas next. We tell more about the topic sentence. Couldn't Shondra just tell about the events in order?

MS. KYOKO: You mean time order? Sure. So what's next, Shondra?

SHONDRA: I guess I tell that there's a trial going on. [*She studies her notes.*] Then I tell about the Fugitive Slave Act. Then about the crowds yelling. And then, after the judge makes the decision, I tell about the fight. [*She pauses.*] Then the headlines.

MS. KYOKO: Perfect. Let's do a rough draft.

> Harriet Tubman showed her boldness at the Charles Nalle Trial. Even though he'd escaped from slavery ten years earlier, Nalle was being returned to his master. The Fugitive Slave Act made the return legal. The crowds outside the courthouse were cheering for Nalle, but Tubman had made plans for his escape. When the judge made his decision, Tubman went into action. She fought with the policemen while Nalle ran out to a waiting wagon. She was "repeatedly beaten over the head with policemen's clubs, but she never for a moment released her hold . . . [and] suffered their blows without flinching." Then she escaped with Nalle. Her bold behavior made headlines in the next day's papers.

SHONDRA: Thanks guys. I'm one paragraph ahead!

MS. KYOKO: True. But the important thing is the process. I wanted you all see how the note cards became the paragraph. And there are a couple of things I want you to notice about this paragraph.

1. As we wrote, we put what's on the note cards into our **own sentences.**
2. Even the quoted part begins with our **own words.**
3. The **quoted words flow into the rest** of the paragraph. You don't say, "Here's a quotation." (We'll add the name of the writer whose words we're quoting later.)
4. **Everything** in the paragraph **says something about the topic sentence.** Everything shows how bold Tubman was.
5. The paragraph uses **time order.**
6. **Connecting words** show how ideas fit together. Words like *even though, but, when, while,* and *then* show time order. They move us from one idea to the next.

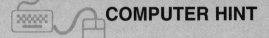

COMPUTER HINT

If you took notes on the computer, and if your software and hardware permit, you can save keyboarding time now. Check these two possible plans:

1. If you saved your notes in separate files by slug, you can now copy files into your first draft. You can move them as needed. Get rid of unneeded words. Then add connecting words, phrases, and sentences. Finally, flesh out the paragraph.

2. If you didn't save notes in separate files by slug, you can use the block move command to move notes into the text of your paper.

Either step keeps you from retyping what's on your note cards.

Remember to make frequent backup files as you work.

JARROD: As usual, Ms. K., you make this look easy. We changed some words, though. Used something different from what's on the note cards.

MS. KYOKO: No problem. In your notes you used abbreviations, like "H.T.," or slang words like "cop." In your report, of course, you spell out "Harriet Tubman" and use "policeman" or "marshall" instead of "cop." Just don't change the words inside quotation marks!

JUAN: This seems clear to me. Is that it for the body of our reports?

MS. KYOKO: Just about. I want to give you one more tip. It will help you keep track of which details came from which source. You'll be taking ideas from your note cards and putting them in your first draft. You don't want to lose track of your **codes.**

JUAN: Oh, that's right. I remember now. When you talked about **plagiarism,** you said we had to tell our audience where ideas came from. If we lose track of the codes, we can't do that.

MS. KYOKO: That's right, Juan. So you need a quick, easy way to keep the codes with the ideas.

JARROD: Okay, coach, give it to us!

MS. KYOKO: It's a secret play, Jarrod. You transfer the code from your note card to your paper. Maybe I can show you rather than tell you. Let's see some of your note cards, Jarrod.

JARROD: No problem. Here are some of the ones about the Ashcroft Trail.

MS. KYOKO: Okay. We have three note cards about the Ashcroft. Let's assume, Jarrod, you're writing a paragraph with these three note cards. Your paragraph could start out something like this:

Canadians felt patriotic following the all-Canadian Ashcroft Trail (10-274). Unfortunately, even though the 125 miles from Vancouver to Ashcroft were easy, the next 1000 miles were awful (4-224-225). In fact, many Canadians felt betrayed. They were misled by the ads that painted such a rosy picture. As one Ashcroft Trail traveler said, "We had been led into a sort of sack, and the string was tied behind us" (4-225).

JUAN: Hey, I see what you did! When you finished writing about what's on a note card, you put the code number right after.

179

Ashcroft - patriotic

10 - 274

Canadians considered selves patriotic
by following all - Canadian route.

Ashcroft - lit. misleading

4 - 224 - 225

Trail not like literature described it.
First 125 mi. OK.
Then 1000 mi. of misery.

Ashcroft - lit. misleading

4 - 225

"We had been led into a sort of sack,
and the string was tied behind us."

MS. KYOKO: That's it. Just don't forget. That code will later become your documentation—the way you tell your readers where you got your details. Now, Shondra, let's go back to your paragraph. Can you put your codes in?

SHONDRA: I think so. [*She compares her note cards with her paragraph; writes.*] How's this?

Harriet Tubman showed her boldness at the Charles Nalle Trial. Even though he'd escaped from slavery ten years earlier, Nalle was being returned to his master. The Fugitive Slave Act made the return legal. (9-13) The crowds outside the courthouse were cheering for Nalle, but Tubman had made plans for his escape. (9-14) When the judge made his decision, Tubman went into action. She fought with the policemen while Nalle ran out to a waiting wagon. She was "repeatedly beaten over the head with policemen's clubs, but she never for a moment released her hold . . . [and] suffered their blows without flinching." (9-15) Then she escaped with Nalle. Her bold behavior made headlines in the next day's papers. (9-15)

MS. KYOKO: Looking good! Now, let me put these three ideas all together for you. First, how paragraphs have main ideas and supporting ideas. Second, how supporting ideas come from note cards. Third, how codes move from note cards to the first draft.

The following pages show how Shondra developed part I-C, "Ignored consequences," of her final outline:

I. Disciplined
   A. Threatened Underground Railroad passengers
   B. Tough on family
   C. Ignored consequences

The following paragraph on page 183 develops part C. (Each lettered part in the outline stands for a paragraph in Shondra's paper.)

II. Creative
   A. Planned escapes
   B. Used disguises
   C. Spied on Rebels

III. Bold
   A. Daring escapes
   B. Nalle trial
   C. Civil War raids

9-55

consequences of discipline

In general, H. T. had "utter disregard of consequences." (She did what she knew to be right — didn't worry about what might happen to her as a result.)

The partial quotation on this note card restates Shondra's topic sentence. (Note how she uses the code 9-55 in her paragraph.)

4-57

slave hunters

Never worried about slave hunters

Reward for her capture reached $40,000.

Shondra's first supporting idea comes from this note card. (Note how she uses the code 4-57 in her paragraph.) This example helps support the topic sentence. It shows Tubman's "not worrying about what might happen to her."

6-164

guerrilla fighter

H. T. = "natural guerrilla fighter" - because of work with underground railroad

Became leader

Knew how to spy, learn secrets.

The idea on this note card introduces Shondra's second supporting idea. She uses this example to explain more about her topic sentence. It also shows that Tubman did not worry about what might happen to her. (Note how Shondra uses the code 6-164 in her paragraph.)

6-112

guerrilla fighter

Her work "created such a total effect in the antebellum period, laying siege, as it did, to the South's fundamental nature — the forceful containment of Negroes in slavery — that the prolonged guerrilla operation can only be called the Battle of the Underground, and it must be compared to the victorious command of a major front in the Civil War itself."

Shondra reduces this long quotation by using the ellipsis. The quotation finishes her second supporting idea. (Note how she uses the code 6-112 at the end of the quotation.)

182

The tough, disciplined Harriet Tubman

did what she did without worrying about what

might happen to her. As one writer put it, she

had "utter disregard of consequences" (9-55).

For instance, she never worried about being

caught by slave hunters, even when the

reward for her hit $40,000 (4-57). Because

she never worried about consequences, she

also became a leader of the guerrilla fighters

(6-164). These were volunteers who sneaked

into Rebel territory, raided the plantations,

and set slaves free. During the Civil War, her

guerrilla plans "created such a total

effect… that the prolonged guerrilla operation

can only be called the Battle of the

Underground, and it must be compared to the

victorious command of a major front in the

Civil War itself" (6-112). Yes, Tubman was

one tough, disciplined woman!

Topic sentence for paragraph explaining "disciplined" (from part I-C of outline)

Connecting words

Connecting words

First supporting idea to explain "not worrying about what might happen to her"

Connecting words

Shondra's own definition to explain "guerrilla fighters"

Connecting words

Second supporting idea to explain "not worrying about what might happen to her"

Ellipsis showing words omitted from original source

Concluding sentence

MS. KYOKO: Well, that puts it all together. Any questions?

JARROD: Yes. I just had this scary thought. It looks to me like everything we write will have to have a code after it.

MS. KYOKO: Almost. You don't have to document anything that is **common knowledge.**

JARROD: What do you mean by "common knowledge"?

MS. KYOKO: Common knowledge is a fact that every source you read agrees on.

CRITICAL THINKING HINT

The easiest way to see if something is common knowledge is to check sources. For instance, every source will agree on the date of Harriet Tubman's death. You won't have to document that. Every source will agree on the route of the three trails into the Klondike. You won't have to document that.

If, on the other hand, you find a certain detail in only one source, then document it.

JUAN: You know, it's funny. You'd think everybody would agree on the habits of a red-tailed hawk. But I found different details in each source.

MS. KYOKO: You mean your sources contradicted one another?

JUAN: No, they just had different kinds of stuff.

MS. KYOKO: In that case, if you find certain details in only one source, document it. Maybe that author is the only one who has proven those details.

JARROD: Well, folks, even I understand this. Anything else, Ms. K.?

MS. KYOKO: We've talked about the beginning and the middle. We haven't talked about the end. Let's look at some ideas about the **end—or the conclusion.**

JARROD: Oops! I almost forgot about the end.

MS. KYOKO: Many students do. They just quit. Every report form, even a video tape or a survey, needs an end. Your audience must feel the topic is covered. Finished.

JUAN: Like knowing the end of the story—how everything turns out.

MS. KYOKO: Good comparison.

SHONDRA: So how do we come up with a good ending?

MS. KYOKO: There are four good ways to conclude a report—in any form.

FOUR WAYS TO CONCLUDE

Give a summary.

Reach a conclusion.

Present a challenge.

Refer to the beginning.

SHONDRA: How about showing us what you mean by these, Ms. K.

MS. KYOKO: Okay. The first is to **give a summary.** In other words, remind your audience what your report said. Wrap up the ideas, but don't just repeat yourself. If you give a summary, Shondra, you will remind your audience of Tubman's military mind. You will probably refer to the three parts of your thesis sentence—discipline, creativity, and bold behavior.

SHONDRA: That works for me.

JARROD: What else, Ms. K.? Personal letters like I'm doing don't usually end in a summary.

MS. KYOKO: True, Jarrod. You can **reach a conclusion.** Pull together the key points to reach an agreement, a decision, a result, or an opinion. Maybe you'll want to show which trail into the Klondike was best.

JARROD: That's possible. What else have other students done?

MS. KYOKO: You could **present a challenge.** Ask your audience to take action. Maybe buy recycled products, write a will, take a class. Or visit the Klondike. Or you might ask them to change an action. Quit smoking, drive more carefully, get more exercise.

JUAN: Somehow I don't see my hawk story in any of these.

MS. KYOKO: Maybe you could **refer to the beginning.** If the beginning had a question, quotation, story, or startling fact, the ending can return to it. Remember the story of Yvette? She was the Russian woman who wanted to buy a loaf of bread. A good ending to that paper would return to Yvette. The concluding story could tell what happens to her in the new Russia.

SHONDRA: That seems to take us full circle. Beginning, middle, and end. Ms. Gant always talks about that when she talks about literature.

JUAN: Good point, Shondra. If I'm doing a story, I guess I should keep that in mind. Wonder how Mr. Mac will like that.

SHONDRA: Well, Ms. K., any other tips before we begin?

MS. KYOKO: Just one reminder. Follow your plan. Work as fast and furiously as you can! Don't worry too much about sentence structure or spelling or punctuation. You can fix all that later. Just get your ideas down!

TIME MANAGEMENT GUIDELINES

The ideal is to create the first draft as quickly as possible. Space the work over several days. Plan to finish a complete part at each sitting. For instance, write in one sitting the three or four paragraphs that will explain one part of your plan. Create in one sitting a map you plan to use. Sketch out in one sitting one letter in a letter file. Allow the following total time for creating your first draft—no matter what the form.

If your report is due in . . .	finish the first draft in . . .
4 weeks	3 days
6 weeks	6 days
8 weeks	8 days
10 weeks	11 days

THREE STUDENTS' PROGRESS

Listen as Shondra, Jarrod, and Juan talk about what happened as they did their first drafts. Their words may help you with your first draft.

187

SHONDRA: When I faced all those note cards and blank pages, I panicked. I've never written anything more than two or three pages. And this is—well, it's kind of hard to tell how long it is. I've crossed out and added. Still, I have 17 pieces of paper. Makes me feel like Superwoman. But I'm getting ahead of myself.

As I said, at first I panicked. Palms sweaty. Couldn't sit still. It was like taking a test I hadn't studied for. I just freak out staring at a blank piece of paper.

I sat flipping through my notes. There was one I really liked. The part about the disguises Tubman used. I thought it was such a funny story about the time she pretended to be reading and hoped the book wasn't upside down. But the disguise worked! The slave catchers thought that old woman couldn't be Tubman—she couldn't read! So I started there.

In other words, I didn't start at the beginning. I started with my second main idea. After I got rolling, I came back to the first idea. And guess when I wrote the introduction? Last! I mean, I'd even done the conclusion before I wrote the introduction! For some reason, I can't do an introduction for a paper I haven't written yet. So my way of writing might seem weird, but it works for me.

Here's the introduction I wrote—after the rest of the paper was in rough draft.

> Most of the world knows Harriet Tubman. She was a conductor of the Underground Railroad. From 1850 to 1861 she made between 15 and 19 trips across the Mason Dixon Line and brought 300 slaves to freedom (1-62, 4-33). In fact, she is one of the ten most unforgettable black women (9-106). What made her so great? She earned the respect of many and made a name for herself as a result of her military mind. As such, she was disciplined, creative, and bold.

I know it needs work. It just kind of drops off after the part about bringing slaves to freedom. I don't know how to get to the part about the military mind. I just stuck the thesis sentence at the end because I know it's supposed to be in the introduction. Ms. K. said not to worry. We'll revise later.

JUAN: I can identify with Shondra. Only, since I write best at the computer, I stared at a blank screen instead of a blank sheet of paper. Same difference.

I ended up spending about two hours a day for three days. But I finished. Just followed my story map. Ms. K.'s suggestion about the map was great. I messed up a couple of times and forgot to put in the number code. Since I didn't throw anything away, though, I was okay. Just went back through my notes and found it. So I don't feel too bad about my report right now.

JARROD: I got busy right away. I started writing. And writing and writing. I worked for an hour every night for a week. I thought I'd never plow through all those note cards. There are still some I didn't use, but Ms. K. says that's okay. We shouldn't force every note into the paper if it doesn't fit, she said.

But my four letters just go on and on. They're too long. Jason read them, and he said they're pretty dull. That they all sound alike. And he says they don't read like friendly letters. And they're confusing.

Here I thought the letters would be so easy to write. Now, after all that work, I'm just sick of it. Besides, we've got this big soccer match Friday night. So I really don't have time to mess with it any more right now. Maybe Jason can help me later. Or maybe you guys can help. These letters need lots of something. And I don't even know what they need.

TIPS AND TRAPS

Every student has a different working style. Some do best at the computer. They know keyboarding, and they type fast. They know how to use the software that makes maps, charts, or brochures. They never have to recopy, only enter changes.

Others write on notebook paper. They cut sections apart, tape them in somewhere else, and reorganize. Others start each new idea on a new page. Follow the style that works best for you.

Two reminders are in order.

Remember to copy the number code from the note card into the rough draft.

You must name the source of every idea and every quotation. If you forget to use the code, you'll lose track of your sources. If you lose track of your sources, you will plagiarize. That is the kind of trouble you want to avoid at all costs.

Remember to stick with your plan.

Of course, if the plan doesn't work, change it. Just stay on track. Answer your guiding question. Do what your thesis sentence says you will do.

CHECKLIST FOR DRAFTING

Your first draft may be of a paper, a chart, a letter, or any of the other 90 forms or combination of forms listed in Chapter 2. In any case, you should be able to answer "yes" to these questions about the draft.

1. Did I work in the style best for me—with pen and paper or with computer software?
2. Did I keep everything, even note cards that seemed not to fit?
3. Does my beginning (or introduction) get the audience's attention?
4. Does my beginning put the audience in the right frame of mind?

5. Does my beginning tell the audience what my report is about (perhaps including the thesis sentence)?

6. Does the middle (or body) follow my plan?

7. Does the middle answer my guiding question (and, therefore, explain my thesis sentence)?

8. Did I use connecting words to show the audience how my ideas fit together?

9. Did I use quotation marks around somebody else's exact words?

10. Did I use number codes to keep track of ideas from every note card?

11. Did I omit note cards that did not fit my final plan?

12. Does the ending (or the conclusion) follow one of the methods for closing my report?

EXERCISES

Exercise A: Thinking about Introductions

Directions: Study the student papers in Chapter 11. Then answer the following questions about beginnings—or introductions.

1. Shondra's introduction takes two paragraphs. What does she do in the first paragraph?

2. What does she do in the second paragraph?

3. Where does she put the thesis sentence?

4. Why do you think her introduction is so long?

5. Juan's introduction is very different from Shondra's. What happens in his first paragraph?

6. Why do you think his introduction is so different?

7. Can you find Juan's thesis sentence? If so, where is it?

8. Jarrod finally decides to write a note to his readers. The note introduces his series of letters. Why do you think he does this?

9. How does Jarrod attract the reader's attention?

10. Can you find Jarrod's thesis sentence? If so, where is it?

Exercise B: Thinking about the Middle

Directions: Study Shondra's paper on pages 244–252. Compare her paper with her plan on page 147. Then answer the following questions about the body of her paper.

1. Name the three main ideas in Shondra's paper.
2. In which paragraph does the first main idea begin?
3. Name the details that explain the first main idea.
4. In which paragraph does the second main idea begin? How can you tell?
5. Name details that explain the second main idea.
6. In which paragraph does the third main idea begin?
7. Name the details that explain the third main idea.
8. What connecting words begin the last paragraph?
9. Does Shondra's paper follow her plan?
10. Which paragraphs in Shondra's paper don't show in her plan?

Exercise C: Thinking about Endings

Directions: Consult the three model papers in Chapter 11. Then, on your own paper, write a response to the following.

1. Name four ways to end a report.
2. Which of these four ways does Shondra use to end her paper?
3. How does Juan end his paper?
4. How does Jarrod end his report?
5. Which ending do you like best? Why?

Exercise D: Now You Write

Directions: Complete the first draft of your own report. Refer to the Checklist on pages 190–191 to remind yourself of important points. When you have a first draft done, go to the Peer Editing Guidelines below.

PEER EDITING GUIDELINES

When you finish your first draft—no matter what its form—ask a peer editor to respond. Ask your peer editor to use the following questions as a guide.

1. What do I like best about the beginning?
2. What could the writer do better in the beginning?
3. What do I like best about the middle—the body—of the report? Why?
4. Which part would I like to know more about?
5. What do I like best about the ending?
6. What could the writer do better in the ending?

PORTFOLIO POINTERS

When your peer editor has answered the questions above, respond to the following questions. Put your peer editor's comments and your response in your portfolio.

1. What do I especially like about my first draft?
2. How can I use what my peer editor said?
3. How could I improve this report?

Chapter 9
Revising the Draft

By now you can almost see how the finished report will look, though it is in a rough form. These last little jobs will polish the rough edges. They will get the report ready for your audience.

MS. KYOKO: So you all have a rough draft now, right?

JARROD: Some of us have rougher drafts than others.

MS. KYOKO: What do you mean, Jarrod?

JARROD: I just can't get mine to work out right. Even Jason says it stinks.

JUAN: Your own brother says it stinks? C'mon, Jarr, it can't be that bad.

MS. KYOKO: Well, I seriously doubt it's anything that we can't fix. How about the rest of you?

SHONDRA: I have all the parts, but I know it needs polish. It's kind of out of shape.

MS. KYOKO: Juan, what about yours?

JUAN: I may be fooling myself, but I don't think mine is all that bad. I mean, I know it's not perfect, but it works. I get from the beginning to the end and tell the hawk's story. Of course, I have an out. The wildlife guy I talked to said he'd read my stuff.

MS. KYOKO: That's great, Juan! A real bonus. Out of courtesy, though, you'll want to share only your best work with him. We'll keep that goal in mind.

JUAN: Good idea.

MS. KYOKO: So, guys, it sounds as if all of you are ready to do some revising. We'll work together on this. Remember that all of us together know more than any one of us alone. If we read one another's reports, we can probably come up with ideas.

JARROD: Can we start with mine? We've got an out-of-town match tomorrow night. I'd like to hear what you guys suggest before I leave. Maybe I can get some work done on the bus.

JUAN: You're dreaming if you think you can work on the bus. But let's see what you have.

JARROD: Okay. I've got these three letters. One for each of the main trails to the gold fields. This fourth letter is like a reply. My brother says they all sound alike, that they're confusing. Too much jammed into them. And they don't read like friendly letters.

SHONDRA: Why don't you give us each a letter and let us read? Okay, Ms. K.?

MS. KYOKO: Sure. I'll take one, too.

JARROD: Great. If you can stand it. I'd rather you guys read it before Ms. Gant rips it apart.

JUAN: [*reading*] Ummm. I see what Jason means. This isn't very friendly.

MS. KYOKO: Juan's right. You know, Jarrod, when you revise, why don't you pretend you're writing to one of us. You've read all about these people. Pretend to be one of them. You can write to us and tell about "your" experiences.

SHONDRA: Another thing. I'm not very good at geography, Jarrod. This letter I'm reading is about the Ashcroft Trail. I don't have any idea where Vancouver and Ashcroft are. Or where the Yukon River is. A map would help me.

JUAN: Good idea. In fact, how about a map that shows all three trails? Then we can compare the three.

SHONDRA: And is one trail more important than another? How many people went on each trail? Did they make it?

JUAN: Yeah, Jarrod. That's important, too. You could put that in a graph.

JARROD: So you want a map and a graph? How will that help the letters?

SHONDRA: Well, they won't help the letters, but they'll sure help the readers. But let me read one or two of the other letters. Maybe we can figure out something for them, too. Let's trade letters. [*They trade.*]

JUAN: Oh, man, this is a looooong letter. Good grief, Jarr, it's six pages. And here's some kind of long list at the end. What's that?

JARROD: Well, everybody who went in had to carry a year's supplies. There was a list. You had to have everything on it—about 2000 pounds of stuff. If you didn't have it, you couldn't cross the border. That's what the list is.

MS. KYOKO: So you think the list is important enough to take up two and a half pages at the end of this letter?

JARROD: Well, I don't know. It seems important to me. No matter which trail stampeders took, they hauled all this stuff. That sure had a lot to do with the problems they faced.

JUAN: Yikes, what a list. I agree it's important. But, Jarr, you said *every* gold rusher had to have the same stuff?

JARROD: Yeah—or the Mounties wouldn't let them into Canada.

JUAN: So the list isn't tied to just this one letter. Right? [*Jarrod nods.*] Then why not make this a separate part of your report?

SHONDRA: Hey, good idea, Juan. This is like a shopping list. Could you do a shopping list?

JARROD: I guess so. I did read that most of the stampeders stopped in Seattle to buy these supplies.

SHONDRA: Well, there! That's your answer. Make this like a sales flier. You know, "Buy here! Best prices in the Northwest!" Something like that.

JARROD: So I'm going to have a map, a graph, a sales brochure, and four letters? You guys are no help.

MS. KYOKO: You said the fourth letter is like a reply to the other three. Do you really need the fourth letter, Jarrod? I don't know, but think about it. Maybe a letter about each of the three trails is enough. What purpose does the fourth letter serve?

JARROD: I'll have to think about that. Maybe you're right. But, hey, guys, thanks a lot. You've really helped me think. Maybe if I write to you, Juan, I'll sound more friendly.

CRITICAL THINKING HINT

Think about each part of your report. Do you, like Jarrod, have ideas that seem not to fit where you have them? Do you need to keep them? Can you put them in another form? Ask your writing group to help. As an audience, they can tell which questions they need answered about your topic.

MS. KYOKO: Okay, what did we learn with Jarrod's paper? Did he follow his plan?

JUAN: He followed his plan. The letters follow the trails the way the people traveled them. It's just that the plan needs some changes.

JARROD: What kind of changes?

JUAN: Just what we talked about. Maybe your letters will work if you add a map. And if you make the list into a sales brochure. And the graph will help. Those weren't part of your plan, but they help answer your guiding question. At least they'll help us!

SHONDRA: They'll also help explain your thesis sentence. But there's something else we learned. Sometimes we just have to say things differently.

MS. KYOKO: You mean write in a different style?

SHONDRA: Yes. I think if Jarrod rewrites these letters as if he's writing to us, they'll work. They're just too stuffy now.

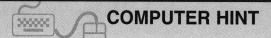

COMPUTER HINT

Some style checkers will check for "stuffy" or "sweet" language. Others will check readability—that is, how easily your paper can be read. These checks may help you know if you are writing to your planned audience.

MS. KYOKO: Good points, all of you. You've learned from Jarrod's work. Now, who else? Shondra?

SHONDRA: Like I said, my paper is just out of shape. I really don't know what it needs.

JARROD: Let's take a look.

SHONDRA: My handwriting is so bad I don't think you can decipher it. I'll read it aloud.

[*She reads.*]

JARROD: I just leaned back and listened. I had to hunt, though, to catch your drift. Somehow it was hard to follow.

MS. KYOKO: Does anybody know why we had trouble following Shondra's ideas? [*Heads shake.*] I think it's because you haven't connected the ideas, Shondra. When you write a long paper, you have to put in lots of connecting words. Sometimes you have to use connecting sentences, or even connecting paragraphs. Let's look at two of your paragraphs. The ones right after your introduction.

Tubman showed her discipline many times. In one case, a runaway slave, tired, cold, and hungry, tried to quit. Tubman pointed a gun at his head and said, "Move or die."

(14-63) "She would allow no one to betray her routes and secrets." (4-50)

When she went back home to take her brothers to freedom, one brother couldn't get there in time because his wife was having a baby. Tubman left him, even though he begged her to wait. Later, when she returned to her parents' house on Christmas Eve, she really wanted to see her mother and father. Tubman's mother never knew her daughter was in the next building. Her father came blindfolded. (6-88)

JUAN: Good details! I can't imagine going off and leaving my brother like that. Or not seeing my folks on Christmas. She was one tough woman.

MS. KYOKO: Juan's right. You have great details to explain how disciplined Harriet Tubman was. What you need is a way to tie the ideas together.

SHONDRA: What do you mean "tie together"?

MS. KYOKO: First, you need an opening sentence for the paragraph. It will show what the first idea has to do with what you said in the introduction. Then you need to explain and connect other ideas. Let me show you. I'll add some sentences and see if you see the difference.

A military mind must be disciplined. Tubman showed her discipline many times. In one case, a runaway slave, tired, cold, and hungry, tried to quit. Tubman pointed a gun at his head and said, "Move or die." (14-63) *She knew that any slave who quit would be beaten until he talked. He would give away her secrets. Her military mind* would allow no one to betray her routes and secrets." (4-50)

Her discipline extended to her family. When she went back home to take her brothers to freedom, one brother couldn't leave in time because his wife was having a baby. Tubman left him, even though he begged her to wait. *She knew they had to leave on schedule or risk being caught. To leave a brother, sister-in-law, and baby she loved, she had to be tough and disciplined.* Later, when she returned to her parents' house on Christmas Eve, she really wanted to see her mother and father. *She knew, though, that her parents could never tell a lie. They could never stand up to questioning by their master. As a result,* Tubman's mother never knew her daughter was in the next building. *She saw her father, but he* came blindfolded. *He could honestly say he never saw his daughter that whole day.* (6-88) *She never let emotion interfere with reason. That is a key to a military mind.*

SHONDRA: Oh, wow, you added a lot! But I see what happened. You told the reader why the examples were important.

JUAN: I see something else. You also repeated some key words, like "tough" and "disciplined." And at the end you came right back to "military mind." That's the whole idea behind your paper, isn't it, Shondra?

SHONDRA: Exactly! Now that I see the idea, I think I can do a better job.

CRITICAL THINKING HINT

Think about why you are using examples. Help your audience see their importance. Show how the details explain your main ideas. Your words must guide the audience's thinking.

MS. KYOKO: I'm glad you see, Shondra. To help you even more, here's a list of some **common connecting words and phrases.** You can refer to the list as you write.

To show time relationships:
after, afterward, at last, at the same time, before, during, earlier, eventually, finally, first, in the meantime, in time, later, meanwhile, next, once, since, soon, then, when, whenever

To show comparison:

again, also, another, as, at the same time, besides, both, each, equally, either . . . or, furthermore, in addition, in like manner, in the same way, like, likewise, moreover, nevertheless, nonetheless, not only . . . but also, similarly, since, still, too, while

To show contrast:

although, but, despite, even if, even though, however, in contrast, in spite of, nor, on the one hand, on the other hand, on the contrary, otherwise, unless, yet

To show degree:

above all, additionally, best, better, even more, further, furthermore, greater, greatest, least, less, more, most, over and above, to a lesser extent, to a smaller degree, worse, worst

To show result or purpose:

as a result, because, consequently, following that, for, in effect, in order that, in the aftermath, next, owing to, since, thus, therefore

To show explanation:

for example, for instance, in fact, in other words, specifically, that is, thus, to be specific, to illustrate

JUAN: I see your point, Ms. K. The connecting words and sentences help the audience stay with you and follow your train of thought.

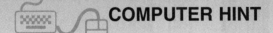

COMPUTER HINT

Some style checkers will highlight and count your connecting words, called "transitions." Although the checker won't recognize connecting sentences, you will find some help in what they do report.

MS. KYOKO: Good points, all of you. Let's make another list. Another summary. This time it's a list of things to think about as you revise. We'll start with what we've just talked about.

CHECK THESE WHEN REVISING

1.   Think about using other forms.

2.   See that your report follows your plan.

3.   Decide if you answer your guiding question.

4.   Show the importance of your examples.

5.   Use connecting words and sentences.

MS. KYOKO: Any questions about these?

SHONDRA: That sums up what we've talked about in our two papers.

MS. KYOKO: Juan, what about you? We haven't seen your paper.

JUAN: I think my paper is okay.

MS. KYOKO: Then let's celebrate by taking a look. [*They read.*]

SHONDRA: Juan, you're right! It's really good. I can feel for that hawk. I never thought I'd say something like that. Not about some dumb bird.

JARROD: He doesn't really need to revise, does he, Ms. K.?

MS. KYOKO: Everybody needs to revise, Jarrod. Just for different reasons. Juan has a form that works for him. He's answered his guiding question. He followed his plan. And he kept his focus on the thesis sentence.

SHONDRA: So what else is there?

MS. KYOKO: Fine tuning. All of you—all of us—need to fine tune. Sometimes I do five or six drafts before I get everything just the way I want it.

SHONDRA: Oh no. If it takes you five or six drafts, I'll never get mine polished.

MS. KYOKO: Of course you will. You have lots of peer readers to help. I don't.

JUAN: What kinds of things should I revise?

MS. KYOKO: Read for **good sentences.** Think about whether you've used different kinds of sentences and sentences of different lengths. Then check **word choice.** See if you've used the same words over and over. Then check for **grammar, usage,** and **mechanics**—things like verb tense, punctuation, agreement. The best way to do that is to use your grammar book for reference. Have your classmates read your paper. Nobody writes something he *knows* is wrong, so you need an objective reader.

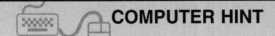

COMPUTER HINT

Some style checkers can be helpful. Most will check spelling and give synonyms and antonyms. Some will count sentence length. Others may highlight connecting words (transitions), linking verbs, and conjunctions. Be warned, though, that style checkers can mislead you. Before you change anything, understand why. Be sure the change is right.

Time Management Guidelines

Although revising takes much less time than writing, it takes more care. If possible, put your report away for a day or so. That lets you come back with a clear mind. As a result, you need to allow some down time as well as revising time. Do not spent more days than the following.

If your report is due in . . .	finish revising in . . .
4 weeks	1 day
6 weeks	2 days
8 weeks	4 days
10 weeks	5 days

Three Students' Progress

As Shondra, Juan, and Jarrod worked on their revisions, they learned some things you may find helpful.

SHONDRA: You already know my biggest job was to get ideas connected. I had to add a lot of explanations in my own words. I needed to tell my audience what was important about the examples I used.

After that, two of my peer editors said I needed to tell a little about Tubman's life. They wanted to know about more than how her mind worked. We tried to figure out

205

how to do that without messing up my plan. Finally Ms. K. said to make the introduction two paragraphs. So I did! I like it lots better now. Seems to give a better look at who Harriet Tubman really was. [See Shondra's complete paper beginning on page 244.] I think it will be a hit with Mr. Koz.

JARROD: I've made lots and lots of changes. I now have a map. It needed an introduction, so I made a legend for it and came up with a title. I found out that's what Ms. K. meant when she said even maps have a beginning, middle, and end!

I also have a sales brochure. That, too, has a front page—the introduction—and two middle pages—the body—with a note on the back giving my source. Juan helped me do it on the computer.

He also helped me do a little graph. It shows how many people traveled each trail—and how many made it. That helps show the problems they faced surviving.

I did the letters over. Three letters now, not four. Each letter tells about the problems on one trail. I tried to put myself in the shoes of the gold seekers and wrote to Juan. That really helped. Having a real audience to write to, I mean. I talked in the letters more like the way I usually talk. The letters work better. Even Jason agrees.

When I had all the letters, the map, and the brochure finished, I took them back to my peer editors. They all said the same thing: Where's the introduction to the project? Each letter has a beginning. The map and brochure have beginnings. The graph has a beginning (title). The whole package needs a beginning.

You know what? That made sense. How else would my audience know how all these pieces fit together? So I wrote an introduction to the project. A letter to my readers. I think it all works now. Thanks to lots of help from my friends!

JUAN: I was really confused when Ms. K. said I needed to do revisions. I thought things were going pretty well. So I stopped by to see her. I had printed out a copy of the first part of my paper, so we worked through one paragraph as an example. Let me show you what happened. Here's the paragraph when we started:

Another day passed. My stomach digested the mouse. It sorted out the food. It separated the garbage, and I spit up the pellet of garbage. I felt hungry again. I wanted to survive, so I had to test my wings. I flew a few feet. It was a clumsy flight. I stopped to rest and tried again. Then I felt stronger. The wounded wing worked more smoothly. Each time I flew just a bit farther. I was thankful the wound wasn't deep. I was almost well.

Ms. K. said my sentences were all pretty much alike. They nearly all started the same way and were all about the same length. She showed me how to make changes. Join sentences. Change the beginnings. Here's what we had when we finished:

After another day, my stomach had digested the mouse and sorted out the food from the garbage. I spit up the pellet of garbage and felt hungry again. If I were to survive, the time had come to test my wings. I flew a few feet, clumsily; stopped to rest; tried again. Each time I felt stronger. Each time the wounded wing worked more smoothly. Each time I flew just a bit farther. I was thankful that the wound was not deep. After yet another day, I was almost well.

I guess there's not much question that I needed to revise! This was really a good lesson for me.

TIPS AND TRAPS

Nobody puts mistakes or poor writing into their report on purpose. One of the best ways to find what needs revising is to ask someone else to read your work. Be careful whom you ask, though. Your best friend may say everything is wonderful because she doesn't want to hurt your feelings. A good peer editor is the best help you can get!

In the end, though, the final job is yours. That means you must read your report for every detail.

CHECKLIST FOR REVISING

No matter what the form (or forms) you use in your report, you should be able to answer "yes" to the following questions.

1. Does my report answer my guiding question?
2. Does it follow my plan?
3. Does it explain my thesis statement?
4. In the written parts, have I written good paragraphs?
   a. Does each paragraph have a good topic sentence?
   b. Do the details explain the topic sentence?
   c. Do the details stick to the topic?
   d. Are the details linked with connecting words?
5. Have I avoided poor grammar, usage, and mechanics?
6. Have I used good, varied sentences?
7. For other forms, have I used clear labels or captions?
8. If I used several forms, have I linked them somehow?
9. No matter the form or combination of forms, have I introduced my report?

EXERCISES

Exercise A: Studying a Paragraph

Directions: Study the following paragraph from a draft of Shondra's paper. Then answer the questions below. As a reminder, reread Shondra's guiding question and thesis sentence.

Guiding Question: What makes Harriet Tubman such a great woman?

Thesis Sentence: Harriet Tubman's military mind made her disciplined, creative, and bold.

In military discipline fashion, she was even tough on her family. When Tubman went home to take her brothers to freedom, one brother was late. His wife was having a baby. Even though he begged her to wait, Tubman left her brother and his wife and baby. To escape, the military planner said they couldn't wait. 5
Later, she showed her toughness again when she returned to her parents' house. It was Christmas Eve. Of course she wanted to see her parents, but she knew that if their master questioned them, her parents could never tell a lie. Thus, Harriet's mother never knew that her daughter was home. Harriet's father 10
brought food, but he was blindfolded so he could honestly say he never saw his children that whole day. Tubman had to be tough to give up seeing her own mother on Christmas. But the military planner stayed tough.

1. What part of Shondra's thesis sentence does this paragraph explain?
2. How does Shondra's topic sentence (the first sentence) help answer her guiding question?
3. How many sentences does Shondra use to give details about this topic sentence?
4. What two examples does Shondra use to explain the topic sentence?
5. What two key words does Shondra repeat several times in the paragraph?
6. Why do you think she repeats these two key words?
7. How does the final sentence refer to the topic sentence?
8. See Shondra's concept web on page 135. Where does this paragraph fit in the web?

Exercise B: Studying Connecting Words

Directions: See the paragraph above from a draft of Shondra's paper. Then answer the following questions about connecting words.

1. Shondra uses two ideas to explain her topic sentence. What group of connecting words in line 2 introduces the first idea?

2. What connecting words do you find in line 3?
3. What connecting words do you find in line 5?
4. What connecting word in line 6 ties together the two ideas that explain Shondra's topic sentence?
5. What other connecting words do you find in line 6?
6. What connecting word do you find in line 7?
7. What connecting word do you find in line 8?
8. What connecting word do you find in line 9?
9. What two connecting words do you find in line 11?
10. What general statement can you make about Shondra's use of connecting words?

Exercise C: Studying Sentences

Directions: Refer to Shondra's paragraph above. Then answer the following questions about the sentences.

1. In which line(s) do you find the longest sentence?
2. In which line(s) do you find the shortest sentence?
3. In which line(s) do you find sentences that start with the subject?
4. In lines 2–3 is a long sentence. It is followed in line 3 by a short sentence. What effect does that have on the reader?
5. In what lines do you find another long sentence followed by a short one?
6. In lines 7–9 is a compound-complex sentence. Why do you think Shondra wrote this as a compound-complex sentence instead of as two shorter sentences?
7. In what lines do you find another compound-complex sentence?
8. In general, what can you say about the sentence variety in Shondra's paragraph?

Exercise D: Now You Write

Directions: Now it's time for you to revise your draft. You may be revising a paper or some other report form. In any case, follow the Checklist on page 208. When you finish your revision, work with a peer editor. (See the Peer Editing Guidelines below.)

PEER EDITING GUIDELINES

Ask a peer editor to read your report with you. Use the Checklist on page 208 as a guide. Then have your peer answer these questions.

1. What is the best part of the report? Why?
2. What part of the thesis statement is explained best? How?
3. What part of the thesis statement would I like to know more about?
4. Does the report follow the plan? If not, should the report be changed or should the plan be changed?
5. Use the Checklist on page 208 as a guide to answer this last question: What should the writer revise?

PORTFOLIO POINTERS

Answer the following questions about your revisions. Then put your answers and your revised paper in your portfolio.

1. What did I learn from making my revisions?
2. What do I especially like about my revisions?
3. How is the revision better than the earlier draft?
4. What problems did I solve as I revised?
5. How can I use what I learned on my next assignment?

Chapter 10

Preparing the Final Report

Y ou've finished a dozen little jobs. You have just one more to do. This last job is to make your report look as good as possible. However, there is more to it than writing neatly in ink or printing out a clean copy. Here are Ms. Kyoko and the students to tell you about it.

MS. KYOKO: Folks, this is it! The finishing touches. Everything you've been doing these last weeks comes together now. You can wow your audience, or you can make them yawn.

JARROD: Leave it to me to make them yawn.

JUAN: Hey, Jarr, c'mon. Where's the old winning spirit?

SHONDRA: Right, you guys. We have only a little more to go. I've worked this hard. I want the final big show to be that—a big show. Appearances might not be everything, but we all know they mean a lot.

MS. KYOKO: You're right, Shondra. I have some hints to give your paper the winning touch. Let's talk first, though, about a detail that has nothing to do with a big show. It has to do with telling where your facts, figures, examples, and ideas come from.

JUAN: Ah, yes. You mean the number codes.

MS. KYOKO: That's right, Juan. We need to break the code for the audience. It's time to give names, dates, places, and pages.

JARROD: Names, dates, places? That sounds like our bib cards.

MS. KYOKO: My, we're sharp this morning! You must have had a good weekend!

JARROD: Yeah, some weekend. I played a miserable game Saturday and slept almost all day Sunday.

MS. KYOKO: Uh, oh. We'll just not talk about it. But maybe Sunday sharpened your mind! At any rate, you're right on target about those bibliography cards. Let's get them out.

SHONDRA: Good thing you told us not to throw anything away. I already had those in my "Trash" envelope.

MS. KYOKO: It would have been a major crisis had you thrown those away!

JUAN: So, how do we decode?

MS. KYOKO: First, let's give this decoding a name. It's called **parenthetical documentation.** Those are big words. They just mean that we put a note in parentheses. That's the "parenthetical" part. The note documents, or names, the sources. That's the "documentation" part. In other words, parenthetical documentation is the note that tells where you found your details.

JUAN: So how do we change the number code to parenthetical documentation? Boy, what a mouthful! Par-en-the-ti-cal doc-u-men-ta-tion. Ten syllables!

MS. KYOKO: It's easier to do than to say. In fact, it's really simple. We substitute the author's or editor's name for the number.

SHONDRA: That's it?

MS. KYOKO: That's it. For instance, say your code is (5-119). Your bib card numbered 5 is a book by Smith. So the note in your paper will be (Smith 119).

JARROD: Wow! That's simple. So when do we use these parenthetical notes?

MS. KYOKO: At two different times. First when you use somebody else's exact words. Second when you use somebody else's ideas.

TWO TIMES TO USE PARENTHETICAL NOTES

1. At the close of a quotation
2. To show the source of ideas

SHONDRA: You know, my paper is (finally!) in my own words. The idea for almost every sentence, though, comes from one of my sources. Does that mean I put a note at the end of every sentence?

MS. KYOKO: Good question, Shondra. Remember, you each did research on something you wanted to learn about—not something you already knew about. You have your own ideas in your introduction and conclusion. You have added your own connecting words and sentences to make the paper smooth.

JUAN: But everything else comes from one of our sources. Right?

MS. KYOKO: Exactly! So there are two general rules about when to use a parenthetical note.

1. **Use a note at the close of every quotation mark.** You must credit exact words right away.
2. **Use a note every time you change sources.** For instance, assume you have a paragraph of seven sentences. The ideas for the first four sentences come from one source. The last three sentences come from another. You'll need two notes. One comes at the end of the fourth sentence. The other comes at the end of the paragraph.

JUAN: What if every one of the seven sentences comes from a different source?

MS. KYOKO: That seems unlikely. But if it happened, you'd use seven notes, one every time you change sources. Let's look at an example. Shondra, let me see a paragraph and your note cards. [*Shondra hands her the materials.*] Okay, as I put this on the board, I'll add the notes you need. [*Writes.*]

At about age thirty, Tubman escaped slavery. Only five feet tall (Chang 12), she soon became a military giant (Colman 62-63). By age forty, Tubman was already called "the General" (Bentley 95). The label stuck. Then during the Civil War, she even "gained the respect of the Union officers" (Bentley 104). In fact, until the 1989 Panama Invasion, Tubman was the only woman—black or white—in American history to lead a military attack ("First Woman" 18).

JUAN: Five parenthetical notes! Are they all necessary?

MS. KYOKO: Yes. Here's why. The first two notes mark ideas from two sources. From Chang you learned that Tubman was five feet tall. From Coleman you learned that she became a military giant. Each time you quit a source you name it. The next two notes are different. They follow words in quotation marks. The quotes are from Bentley. Every time you close a quotation, you put a note to show where the words came from. The last note is from an article titled, "First Woman."

JARROD: But you have Bentley in there twice. Why not just wait until you finish with Bentley? You know. Use one note.

MS. KYOKO: Good question. Just remember, you use a note at the close of every quotation. Bentley is quoted twice, so you have to have two notes.

JARROD: That sure looks funny.

MS. KYOKO: Maybe so, but that's the way it's done. And there's another strange-looking thing about notes. We already said that when you quit a source and go to another, you name the source, right?

JUAN: Right.

MS. KYOKO: Now, if you come back to that same source a sentence later, you name it again when you leave it.

SHONDRA: Could you show us what you mean?

MS. KYOKO: Of course. Juan, let's see your draft. [*He hands her his paper.*] Ah, here! Take a look at this. [*She writes a paragraph on the board.*]

> Finally, on the sixth day, I caught a thermal. It's like a swirling doughnut of warm air that rises as the sun warms the air near the ground (Switzer 14). I soared! My fifty-inch wing span (Ripper 14) and fan-like tail typical of us buteos once again put me a mile high. With eyes ten times stronger than humans', I watched for rodents on the ground (Switzer 11, 5). If humans only understood that they and we are not after the same game! My favorite food is limited almost entirely to rodents (Ripper 10).

JARROD: You guys, this is making me nervous. Switzer, Ripper, Switzer, Ripper. What's the deal?

MS. KYOKO: Everything in this paragraph is from Switzer or Ripper. The part about the thermal comes from Switzer. The part about the fifty-inch wing span comes from Ripper. Juan needs notes after both parts.

JARROD: Oh, I get it! Then he comes back to Switzer for the stuff about the tail, the mile-high flight, and the eyes. Then back to Ripper about the favorite food. So it's a note every time we finish one source and turn to another.

MS. KYOKO: Bingo! That's it exactly.

SHONDRA: I guess there are rules about **punctuation** and all that good stuff?

MS. KYOKO: You guessed it. Start the note one space after the quotation mark. Put the period, question mark, or exclamation point after the note. Like this:

> Tubman was, according to John Brown, "a better officer than most" (Conrad 120).

JARROD: What if the quotation isn't at the end of a sentence?

MS. KYOKO: You'll put the note at the close of the quotation. Like this:

> Some say that "of the 5000 men who tried [the White Pass trail], . . . scarcely 500" (Berton 84) made it.

JARROD: What if we just use an idea, not someone's exact words?

MS. KYOKO: In that case, start the note one space after the last word of the sentence. Put the period, question mark, or exclamation point after the note. Like this:

> Folks can't take horses up the Chilkoot, so they take the White Pass. Sad to say, it's a death trap (Hunt 46).

JUAN: I can think of all kinds of exceptions. Like what if we have two authors?

SHONDRA: Right. Or a magazine article without an author?

JARROD: Or more than one book by the same author. What then?

MS. KYOKO: Good questions. If you have **two authors or editors,** use both last names. If you have **no author or editor,** use the title. If you have **more than one source by the same author,** use the name and the title. Here. Let's put all that in an easy-to-read chart.

Writing Problem Notes

PROBLEM	SOLUTION	PUNCTUATION	EXAMPLES
Two authors or two editors:	Use both last names.		(Jones and Hopkins 143)
More than two authors or editors:	Use only the first last name, followed by "and others."		(Collins and others 221)
No author or editor:	Use the title, shortened if possible.	Use quotation marks or underscore for title.	("Working Mothers" 16)
More than one work by the same author:	Use both the author name and the title, shortened.	Separate the author's name from the title with a comma.	(Burton, *Gold Rush* 308)

JUAN: That all seems clear enough. What's next?

MS. KYOKO: We'll do the list of works cited.

JARROD: Oh, I remember talking about that. It's a list of all our bib cards, right?

MS. KYOKO: Yes. To begin, pull out the bib cards of sources you did not use. Put them in your "trash" envelope.

JUAN: That's easy. I used all but two of mine.

MS. KYOKO: All right. Next put the bib cards in **alphabetical order.**

SHONDRA: Okay, that's easy. I have some I don't know what to do with, though. How do we alphabetize things without an author or editor?

MS. KYOKO: Alphabetize those by the title of the article. Use whatever is on the first line of your bib card.

SHONDRA: Oh, that's right. We indented all but the first line of the bib cards. Hanging indentation, you called it. That's so we could alphabetize easily.

JARROD: I have another question. I have three books by the same author. Does it matter what order I put them in?

MS. KYOKO: Yes, alphabetize those by the title. If the title begins with an article (*A, An,* or *The*), ignore it and alphabetize by the next word.

JARROD: I think we're okay on alphabetizing. What's next?

MS. KYOKO: The **Works Cited page.** It's just an alphabetical list of your bib cards. You'll type it up on a page—or maybe two. That will be the last page (or pages) of your report.

SHONDRA: Do we use the same form on the Works Cited page as we did on the bib cards?

MS. KYOKO: Yes. There are some special rules for this page (or pages). Let's look at them.

JUAN: Wait a minute before you get too far into this. Does everybody have to do a Works Cited page? I'm not doing a paper like Shondra's. Neither is Jarrod. So do we still have to do this page?

MS. KYOKO: Absolutely. True, the forms of your reports differ. But everyone must list the sources they used.

JARROD: Nice try, Juan. Okay, let's get the details. I'll need to write this all down. Otherwise I won't remember.

MS. KYOKO: That's right, Jarrod. There are eleven little rules. Here we go.

1. Center the words "Works Cited" one inch from the top of the page. Do not use quotation marks. Do not punctuate it in any way. Capitalize the first letter of each word.

2. Double-space everything on the page.

3. Begin the first entry one double space below the title.

4. Begin each entry at the left margin. Indent all other lines five spaces.

5. Use the same form as for bibliography cards. (See Chapter 5 and model Works Cited pages in Chapter 11.)

6. List sources in alphabetical order by the first word on your bibliography card. That will be either the author's or editor's last name or the title of the article or book. If a title begins with *A*, *An*, or *The*, alphabetize by the next word.

7. Underline titles of books and magazines. Put quotation marks around titles of articles.

8. Every parenthetical note in your text must have a reference on the Works Cited page.

9. If you use two or more sources by the same author, follow these rules:
   a. List the author's name in the first entry.
   b. In following entries, use three hyphens followed by a period.
   c. Arrange the publications in alphabetical order by title.

Examples:

> Steinhart, Peter. "No Net Loss." <u>Audubon</u> July 1990:1821.
> ---. "Standing Room Only." <u>National Wildlife</u> April-May
> 1989: 46+.

10. Keep a one-inch bottom margin.

11. Use more pages as necessary. Do not use the "Works Cited" title on further pages. Begin the text one inch from the top.

SHONDRA: Wow! There are lots of rules. Sounds hard.

MS. KYOKO: It isn't really hard. It's just that research demands an eye for detail. The detail includes how you show your work to an audience. [See Shondra's, Juan's, and Jarrod's completed Works Cited pages in the next chapter.]

JARROD: Speaking of detail, I remember when Jason did his final draft. There were lots of rules for the final paper. You're going to tell us about that, right?

MS. KYOKO: Right! What you're talking about is called **manuscript form.** Keep in mind that what we'll be talking about applies mostly to written forms. If you're using another form, apply the ideas toward neatness.

JARROD: Okay, a step at a time. Tell us about the written forms. After that, I might have questions about the other parts of my report.

MS. KYOKO: Good plan, Jarrod. So here we go. First, most final drafts are done on a typewriter or a computer-fed printer. That's true even of written parts of other forms like captions for photographs, legends for maps or graphs, or introductions to reports that include several forms. Sound familiar, Jarrod?

SHONDRA: What if we don't have a typewriter or computer?

MS. KYOKO: If you must write in longhand, use blue or black ink. Write on only one side of the paper. No matter how you do your final draft, however, certain rules apply. Let's talk about paper and print.

PAPER AND PRINT

1. Use 8 1/2" × 11" white paper. Type or print on only one side. Do not use paper labeled "erasable"; most inks smear on it.

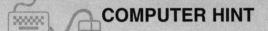

COMPUTER HINT

If you have a continuous-feed printer, use finely perforated paper (sometimes called "microperf"). When the tractor-feed strips are torn off, very smooth edges remain. The paper is readily available in computer stores and office supply stores.

If your printer has a sheet feeder, use twenty-pound typing paper for best results.

2. Always make a copy of your paper and keep it. The copy may be a carbon copy, a photocopy, or, for computer users, another printout.
3. Use a crisp black ribbon. Avoid other colors. Clean the striking keys on your typewriter so that letters (especially *o*'s and *e*'s) are not blobs on the paper.
4. For the body of your report, use plain type. Avoid fancy type, like *italics*. You may be able to use other type sizes or styles. They can set off headings, captions, and other short pieces of text. Ask your teacher first.
5. With a typewriter, avoid strikeovers. Avoid using erasers that can rub holes in the paper. Use, instead, correcting ribbon, lift-off tape, or correcting fluid.

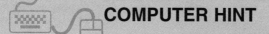

COMPUTER HINT

Given a choice, use a letter-quality printer rather than a dot-matrix printer.

Do *not* justify the right margins of a research paper. Other forms, like a newspaper, may require justified right margins. Compare the following two paragraphs.

This paragraph is written *without* a justified right margin. We refer to this as a "ragged right" margin. Most student papers should be written with ragged right margins.

This paragraph is written *with* a justified right margin. By that we mean that the right margin is straight. Computer programs adjust the letters across the page to make the right margin even.

JARROD: Those seem like commonsense things. Is that what we're doing here?

MS. KYOKO: In many ways, yes. Good writers show respect for their audiences. As a result, they want anything they've written to look inviting and easy to read.

JUAN: That's like a computer program being called "user friendly."

MS. KYOKO: Good comparison! You want your research reports to be "audience friendly." So here are a few more hints for making the report look friendly.

General Appearance

1. Avoid dividing words at the ends of lines. Ragged right margins are okay and make life easier for your reader.

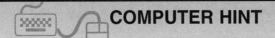

COMPUTER HINT

If your word processing software has an automatic hyphenation feature, turn it off. You will have one less problem to check (especially since automatic hyphenations are sometimes wrong).

2. Double-space the entire paper. That includes the Works Cited page(s) and outline page (if used).
3. Use one-inch margins on all four sides of the paper.
4. When starting a new paragraph, always have at least two lines at the bottom of a page. When ending a paragraph, always have at least one full line and part of another at the top of a page.

COMPUTER HINT

Your word processing software may let you automatically stop widows (single lines at the tops of pages) or orphans (single lines at the bottoms of pages). If not, preview pages before you print and force page ends as necessary.

SHONDRA: Those rules don't seem hard to follow. I'm thinking ahead, though. When we start the first page, do we have a title and our names and then start writing?

MS. KYOKO: Not exactly. The first page has some information that tells about you, your class, and your paper. Let's look at those details.

The First Page

A regular research paper does not require a title page. Instead, certain items appear on the first page of the text:

1. At the right margin, a half-inch from the top, put your last name and the number 1, like this: Johnson 1. This is called the "running head."
2. At the left margin, one inch from the top, on four double-spaced lines, write
    — your name
    — your teacher's name
    — the course title
    — the date in day/month/year order
3. One double space below, center your title. Do not underline it or use quotation marks. Capitalize the first letters of main words.
4. Continue to double-space after the title and begin your text. Indent five spaces for each paragraph.

On page 244 is the first page of Shondra's paper. It illustrates each of the above rules about how first pages should look.

JARROD: You said this first page format is for regular papers. Juan and I are doing other forms. Do we do something different?

MS. KYOKO: Yes. For other forms, use a title page. It really ties together the parts of your report. In other words, it says to your audience, here's a research report about the Klondike.

JARROD: Oh, I see. Otherwise, they start reading my letters cold. They have no idea what they're getting into.

MS. KYOKO: Exactly! So, for those, you need a title page. We'll talk about that next.

Neal 1

Shondra Neal
Gerald Kozloski
Social Studies
18 January 19--

Harriet Tubman: Military Giant

Most people know about Harriet Tubman. She was a conductor on the Underground Railroad. From 1850 to 1861 she made almost twenty trips across the Mason Dixon Line and helped 300 slaves to freedom (Ferris 62, McCarty 33). But there's much more to know about Tubman. In fact she is one of the ten most unforgetable black women (Norment 106). What makes her so unforgetable?

At about age thirty, Tubman escaped slavery. Only five feet tall (Chang 12), she became a military giant (Colman 62-63). By age forty, Tubman was already called "the General" (Bently 95). The label stuck. Then, during the Civil War, she even "gained the respect of the Union Officers" (Bently 104). In fact, until the 1989 Panama Invasion, Tubman was the only woman--black or white--in American history to lead a military attack ("First Woman" 18). Why was she "General" Tubman? Her military mind earned her the label. That military mind made her disciplined, creative, and bold--a hero.

Any paperback war hero must be disciplined. General Tubman was such a hero. Once as she led some runaway slaves to freeman, one man grew tired, cold and hungry. He wanted to give up. Like a general in battle, Tubman pointed a pistol

The Title Page

If your report is something besides a paper, you may need a title page. (Follow your teacher's advice.) Use this guide to create a title page.

1. Keep two-inch margins on all four sides of the title page. Center the material from left to right on the page. Balance it from top to bottom.
2. Make three parts to the title page, as follows:
3. In the first part, give the title. Capitalize the first letter of each main word. Do not underline. Do not use quotation marks. Do not end with a period.

4. For the second part, skip three double spaces. Then write "by" in lowercase letters. Do not punctuate.

5. Skip a double space. Write your name. Capitalize only the first letter of each part of your name.

6. For the third part, skip three double spaces to give
   — name of course
   — teacher's name
   — date in day/month/year order
   Double-space between each.

Below is the title page from Jarrod's research report. It models the rules above. Follow it if you must use a title page with your report.

```
                  Trails to the Klondike




                           by

                    Jarrod Johnson




                      English 1

                      Ms. Gant

                  24 January 19--
```

SHONDRA: Lots of details! When we get past the first page, the rest goes without a hitch, right?

MS. KYOKO: That's almost right. There are only few details we haven't talked about. Let's look at them now.

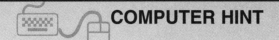

COMPUTER HINT

Most word processing software has a centering command. It will automatically center a line of text from left to right. Many programs also center text from top to bottom. Both commands will speed the job of making a neat title page.

Getting the Details Right

Whether you use a title page or not, follow the rest of these details.

1. On each page following the title page, use a running head. Place it a half inch from the top and one inch from the right margin.
2. Begin text on all pages one inch from the top.

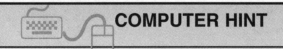

COMPUTER HINT

Most word processing software has an automatic numbering function. If yours does, give a command at the beginning of the file to run a header on every page at the flush-right margin. Create a header that gives your name and page number. You won't have to think about it anymore.

The following page from Shondra's paper models the running head and top spacing for the pages of a report.

Neal 2

at his head and said, "Move or die" (Colman 63). Any slave
who tried to run away but gave up would be beaten until he
talked. Tubman "would allow no one to betray her routes and
secrets" (Taylor 50). It took a tough woman to threaten to
kill a fellow runaway.
   In military style, she was even tough on her family.
When Tubman planned to take her brothers to freedom, one
brother was late. His wife was having a baby. Even though he
begged Tubman to wait, military discipline would not let her.
Months later, she returned home and showed the same
discipline. It was Christmas Eve. She really wanted to see
her parents, but she knew if their master questioned them,
her parents could never lie. So Harriet's mother never knew
her daughter was home. Harriet's father brought food, but he
was blindfolded. That way, he could honestly say he never saw
his children the whole day (McClard 88). Tubman's discipline
helped her give up seeing her family on Christmas.

---

3. If you use a quotation longer than four lines, use the
    following format:
    a. Begin the long quotation on a new line.
    b. Indent all lines of the quotation ten spaces from the
       left margin. Keep the one-inch right margin. Double-
       space.
    c. Do not use quotation marks before or after the long
       quotation. By indenting, you have already shown the
       words are quoted.
    d. Put a parenthetical note after the last punctuation
       mark.
    e. Begin a new line to continue text. Do not indent un-
       less the new line is also a new paragraph.
4. If you use a quotation that is less than four lines, run it
    in with the rest of the text, and put quotation marks
    around it.

The following page from Jarrod's report shows a long quotation and short quotations. It models the rules above about writing quotations. Use it as a guide when you use quotations in your own research report.

---

lots of fellows never tended a horse before and don't know head from tail. It'd make you sick to see the way some animals were treated. "One man was jabbing at his horse's flanks with a knife to make him keep moving. The creature hobbled to the edge of a precipice, looked down for a moment, and deliberately jumped" (Poynter 64-5). There was also a horse that had broken its leg

> where the trail squeezed between two huge boulders. The horse's pack had been removed, and someone had knocked it on the head with an ax; then traffic was resumed directly across the still warm body. . . . That evening there was not a vestige of the carcass left, save for the head on one side of the trail and the tail on the other. The beast had literally been ground into the earth by the human machine. (Berton, Fever 155)

A man up here named Jack London said it all: "Their hearts turned to stone--those which did not break--and they became beasts, the men on the Dead Horse Trail" (Berton, Rush 187). I'll never forget what I saw. I'm ashamed of the human race for what happened on that 45 miles of switchback trail.

But I think things are better now. I hear they've built a railroad through the White Pass.

Yours truly,

Jed

SHONDRA: Does that finish the final draft?

MS. KYOKO: Yes. Those are the details for preparing the final draft. But you remember the writing process. What's the one thing we haven't talked about?

JARROD: We talked about revising. But we didn't say any-thing about proofreading.

MS. KYOKO: That's it! And proofreading takes time. Save at least one whole evening for it. Better yet, get a buddy and proofread each other's papers. You know, nobody writes some-thing that's wrong on purpose. It's much easier to see some-one else's mistakes than your own.

JUAN: What do we look for when we proofread? The usual—spelling, grammar, stuff like that?

MS. KYOKO: Yes. Let's put it in a list. Then you and your peer editor can check each other's papers against it.

Proofreading—Grammar, Mechanics, and Usage

1.   Read slowly to catch missing words and other common errors. Try reading aloud to a friend or to yourself.

COMPUTER HINT

Proofread from the printed copy, not just from the screen. Errors are easier to see on paper.

2.   Look for typing errors, especially three common ones:
    a. Transposed letters. It's easy to type *autunm* instead of *autumn*. And it's hard to see in a quick reading.
    b. Missing letters. Reading quickly, you'll miss the error in *suceed*.
    c. Wrong letters. You might type *then* instead of *than*.
3.   Check spelling. To misspell is to insult your audience.
4.   Read for punctuation. Three tips:

a. Check compound and compound-complex sentences. Watch for run-ons and comma splices. Use a handbook.
b. Avoid the advice to "punctuate where you pause." Punctuate by the rules.
c. Check punctuation marks used with quotation marks. Periods and commas go inside quotation marks. Semicolons go outside. Question marks and exclamation points go inside if they are part of the quotation.

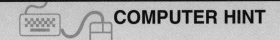

COMPUTER HINT

You may like using a computer spell checker. It's often part of your word processing software. A word of warning: Don't expect it to find all your errors. As long as a word is spelled right, a spell checker will not find a wrong word. It does not know that you meant to say *out* instead of *our.* Even with a spell checker, you must still read your report carefully.

5. Check for common grammatical errors: subject-verb agreement and pronoun-antecedent agreement. Use a handbook.
6. In a formal paper, get rid of contractions, slang, and colloquialisms. You can use them in interviews, skits, and other forms that need conversation-like language.

COMPUTER HINT

Several computer programs check grammar and style. Use them with care. They are not foolproof. (Most even give the Gettysburg Address a poor rating.) Grammar and style checkers are best for writers who know the rules and how to use them. Be alert.

SHONDRA: What about students who don't have a regular paper? Maybe they have just audio stuff. How can they proofread?

MS. KYOKO: Everybody has a Works Cited page or pages. That, too, must be proofread. And checking it means careful letter-for-letter, punctuation-mark-for-punctuation-mark attention. These steps will help:

Proofreading the Documentation

1. Check the Works Cited page for mechanical errors. Check carefully. This page uses rules for capitalization, commas, periods, quotation marks, underscoring. (See the Works Cited pages for the model papers in the next chapter.)
2. Check the Works Cited page for alphabetical order. (See Chapter 9 for the rules.)
3. Check the use of exact words in your report. Compare note cards with the final paper. Check for quotation marks, beginning and ending, around exact words.
4. Check for accuracy. Check spelling. Check page numbers.
5. Check that every parenthetical note has an entry on the Works Cited page.

JARROD: Whew! We have a lot of details to check. All of us! But then we're finished. We just turn in the report and wait for the worst.

MS. KYOKO: [*Laughing.*] Well, I hope it's not the worst, Jarrod. Before you turn in the report, though, ask your teacher how he wants it put together.

JUAN: What do you mean "put together"?

MS. KYOKO: Your teacher may want you to use only a paper clip to hold all the pages and parts together. On the other hand, he may want you to use a binder. I've know some teachers who wanted rather formal covers on reports.

SHONDRA: I can't believe it, you guys. We're on the last little job. The last one! Yes!

Time Management Guidelines

The final report shows what you have worked hard to gather and put together. Sloppy work now makes all the work you've done for these past weeks look bad. So you want to take care to put together a good-looking report. That is true no matter what form or forms you use.

The time you need for the final draft depends on how you did your earlier drafts. If you did your drafts at the computer, you will only do fine tuning. That won't take long. If you wrote everything by hand and you are a hunt-and-peck typist, you will need several hours. The timeline below assumes you fall somewhere in between. Adjust accordingly.

If your report is due in . . .	finish your final draft in . . .
4 weeks	3 days
6 weeks	4 days
8 weeks	5 days
10 weeks	7 days

Three Students' Progress

Before we see their three papers, listen to your friends Shondra, Juan, and Jarrod one last time. Think about your own report as they tell what happened when they prepared their final products.

SHONDRA: This is it! The stress is on. And that's when I make mistakes. Thank goodness I started early getting this final draft typed. I'm not a fast typist, so I spent two or three hours on four evenings to get done.

My best friend uses an old portable typewriter. She nearly went nuts. First of all, she doesn't type well. So she made lots of mistakes. She had no correcting ribbon. Finally she resorted to "white out." You've seen it—that stuff you paint over errors and then retype. Now her paper looks diseased. Twice she forgot to put the parenthetical notes in. So she had to retype the whole page. Another time she was thinking so hard about typing without mistakes that she typed too close to the bottom of the page. She had to retype that page, too. Boy! Was she ever stressed out!

I guess the hardest part for me was just getting done. It took longer than I thought it would. My best advice? Get started as soon as you can. After all, who wants to fall short on the last day and mess up the whole project? It's worth thinking about.

JUAN: Since I did all my work at the computer, the final form was a breeze. I had to change the first page to put in my name, class, and date. And I had to add the running heads. The biggest job for me was doing the Works Cited page. You know, making sure all the commas and periods were right. That the spacing was right. That I capitalized or underlined or put in quotation marks in the right places.

Oh, one really interesting thing happened as I worked on my final draft. You'll remember Ms. K. said I needed a picture of a red-tailed hawk. I was going to make a photocopy of one from a book and put that in my report. You know, give credit and all. Do it right. But when the wildlife guy read my report, he said I should take my own picture. Make it first class. Well, I can't go find a hawk and take pictures. Not where I live. But he had the answer. Take a picture of the mounted hawk in the nature center! So that's what I did. Since I'm taking a photography class at school, it all fit together.

So there's this new part to my report. A portrait. I did a slight revision to refer to "my portrait" in the narrative. The whole idea really added a neat touch to my report. I think Mr. Mac will be impressed. At least I hope so.

The whole point is that even while you're doing your final draft, things may change! It's never too late to add something that will make the report better.

JARROD: I did my final draft at the computer in the school media center. I don't have a computer at home. So until this project, I had done everything with pen and paper. With Juan's help, I figured out how to do a brochure. That was a nice little touch to my project. Thank goodness Juan reminded me! I forgot about the parenthetical note on the brochure. That list of supplies was copied almost word for word from one of my sources. I'd have been in big trouble if I'd left out the credit! It's easy to forget to put credit notes on maps, brochures, pictures, charts—things like that.

It's funny, but doing the final manuscript seems to mean that Murphy's Law kicks in. You know, the one that says anything that can go wrong will? Shelly and Samantha, two girls in my class, were working together at Samantha's house. Samantha has a computer. They figured they could finish in one evening, so they waited until the night before the report was due.

Well, something weird happened to the computer. Samantha's dad finally got things working again. Then they couldn't get the printer to do a running head. Because they wasted so much paper trying to get the page numbers right, they ran out of paper. By then the stores were closed. They were calling all around at midnight trying to find paper. Finally they had to write their papers out by hand to have them ready the next morning for class.

I guess the lesson is simple. Expect that Murphy's Law will kick in. Don't wait until the last minute to do your final draft!

My big problem? Trying to get all the parts of my report to fit together. When I showed my draft to Mr. Koz, he said I needed an introduction. That's what you guys told me, but I hadn't done it. Mr. Koz said to give a little background. Tell who the letters were from. Refer to the map.

After I did all that, Jason said to add a title page. That seemed to make it all fit together. I know Ms. K. said we all needed an introduction. But I thought if each letter had a beginning that would be enough. Not so! The whole report needs an introduction. Jason thinks it's a good report now. I hope Mr. Koz agrees!

I've really learned a lot about all kinds of things. The Klondike, letter writing, report writing, using the computer. And most of all I've learned a ton about doing a research report! It's no mystery for me any more!

TIPS AND TRAPS

Student research writers often fall into the same traps. Listen to these students as they give tips to keep you from making the same mistakes.

JOYCE: I did my first research report three years ago. I've done two more since then. I can assure you of one thing. Murphy's Law *will* be in effect. Anything that can go wrong will. You have to learn that typewriters, computers, and printers break down at the last hour. Assume you will run out of something—even if it's only patience. Why do I tell you all of this? It's a warning. Allow plenty of time to do your final draft!

LORENZO: Joyce and I were in the same class. I can add another tip. Remember that the final draft needs to look super. Pay attention to details. Try to make charts, maps, drawings—whatever—look good. Really good. If you have to draw your own graphs or maps, use black ink. When you can, use the typewriter or computer-fed printer for labels, captions, and little stuff. Then paste them down neatly.

LUIS: Lorenzo is right. You want everything to look really good. When I did my first research report, I needed to put in some charts and graphs. I hunted up some samples in my math and social studies books. Then I modeled mine after them. So I can add one more tip: Hunt up models to help you see what some special form should look like.

Chapter 2 lists about ninety forms you can use for your report. Of course, all ninety models are not shown, but they're easily available. The best models are in books, periodicals, and other published media. If, for instance, you're writing a script for a play, look in your literature book for a model. If you're writing an advertisement, look in your newspaper or your mailbox for a model. If you're making a video tape, look to your television for a model. If you are designing a chart, graph, or map, look in your social studies book for a model.

CHECKLIST FOR PREPARING THE FINAL DRAFT

You should be able to answer "yes" to the following questions about your final draft.

1. Have I put everything on 8 1/2" × 11" paper unless the form (like a poster or newspaper) suggests another size?
2. Did I use crisp, black print?
3. Have I double-spaced all text, including the Works Cited page?
4. Did I use one-inch margins on all four sides of my report?
5. If my report includes several forms, did I use a title page?
6. Are the three parts of the title page centered?
7. After the title page, did I format the first page with a running head and title?
8. If my report requires it, did I use a table of contents or outline?
9. If my report does not require a title page, did I format the first page with a running head and title? Does it include the following on separate lines at the left margin?
   (a) my name
   (b) the teacher's name
   (c) the class title
   (d) the date in day/month/year order

10. Beginning with page 1, have I used a running head at the right margin, a half inch from the top?

11. Did I set off quotations more than four lines long?

12. Did I use a parenthetical note every time I used someone else's exact words?

13. Did I use parenthetical documentation each time I changed sources?

14. Have I used the right form, spacing, and punctuation for documentation?

15. If necessary, have I used ellipses correctly?

16. If necessary, did I use brackets correctly?

17. Is the Works Cited page formatted correctly?
    (a) Does it have a running head?
    (b) Does it have a title?
    (c) Did I use hanging indentation for each entry?

18. Did I punctuate all the entries properly?

19. If I used more than one work by the same author, did I use the following pattern on the Works Cited page?
    (a) The first entry lists the author's name.
    (b) All other entries begin with three hyphens followed by a period.
    (c) The works are alphabetized by title.

20. Did I make a copy of my report?

EXERCISES

Exercise A: Studying Final Reports

Directions: The final research reports by Shondra, Jarrod, and Juan are in the next chapter. Refer to them to answer the following questions.

1. Look at the first page of Shondra's report on page 244. What is the first source she names?

2. Find that source in the Works Cited list. From what book or magazine does that source come?

3. How many sources did Shondra use to write her first three paragraphs?
4. Look at the first page of Shondra's paper. What does she include in the running head?
5. What four items does she list at the left margin?
6. What is different about the way the date is listed?
7. Look at the beginning of Jarrod's paper on page 266. He uses a title page. What three parts does the title page have?
8. Why does Jarrod need a title page while Shondra does not?
9. Look at page 3 of Shondra's paper. One quotation uses a series of periods: "effect . . . that." What do the periods mean?
10. Look at Juan's Works Cited list on pages 263–264. How many sources did he use to write his paper?
11. In what order are the sources listed?
12. Something is underlined in almost every source listed. What kind of works are underlined?
13. Does Juan list any magazines or periodicals?
14. When Juan lists a book with two or three authors or editors, how is the first author's name written? How are the other names written?
15. How many "little sentences" (that is, groups of words followed by a period) do you find in each entry?

Exercise B: Practicing Proofreading

Directions: The following sentences are from a research report about above-ground coal mining. This part talks about the problems that bad weather causes. The sentences are numbered. Each has the kinds of errors you should correct when you proofread. Most sentences have more than one error. Correct the errors.

1. Severy cold effect miners the same way it effect everyone, but on a much greater scale.
2. Its hard to dig in frozen ground.
3. As a result: mining was seriously slowed.

4. The machinery become so stiff that it doent work.

5. For instance, even with 180 tons of coal baring down on the unloading doors they won't open and the coal can't be unloaded.

6. Sometimes the cole freezes in the trucks or on the conveyor lines in the preparation plant.

7. Then men must use pick axes to brake up the frozen mass, such work also seriously slowed the job.

8. While cold is bad, rain is worst.

9. The minning pits may fill with water and have to be pumbed out.

10. The roads become soupy pathes with much several feet thick, sticky much that drys to boots like concreet.

Exercise C: Now You Write

Directions: Use the Checklist on pages 238–239 to check your own final report. Make final corrections as necessary.

PEER EDITING GUIDELINES

When you finish your final report, ask a peer editor or someone from your writing group to look at it. Ask him or her to use the Checklist on pages 238–239 to react to your final report.

PORTFOLIO POINTERS

Now that your final report is done, think back over the process of creating your report. Answer these questions. Put your answers in your portfolio.

1. What did I learn about my topic?
2. What are three things I learned about doing a research report?

3. What part of the research process (finding a topic, finding sources, taking notes, writing the draft, revising the report) did I do best?
4. What part of the research process was hardest for me?
5. If I could start over with this research project, what would I do differently? Why?
6. How can I apply what I learned to my next research report?

Chapter 11
Studying Three Model Reports

You have followed Shondra, Jarrod, and Juan as they worked. You heard about their first fears. You heard their questions. You learned about their problems. You heard them talk about what worked (and didn't work) for them.

Now you are about to see their finished reports. The reports are very different from each other. Shondra's is a traditional written report. Jarrod's is a letter file; however, it also has a brochure, a graph, and a map. Juan's is a story told in first person. He included a photograph. Later, at his teacher's suggestion, he changed it into a hypermedia report. You'll see his flow chart for that.

All reports have the two parts of documentation needed for a research report: parenthetical documentation and a list of works cited.

Shondra, Jarrod, and Juan hope you liked sharing their experiences, and that they have helped you make your report as good as theirs are!

Shondra Neal

Gerald Kozloski

Social Studies

18 January 19-

Harriet Tubman: Military Giant

Most people know about Harriet Tubman. She was a conductor on the Underground Railroad. From 1850 to 1861 she made almost twenty trips across the Mason Dixon Line and helped 300 slaves to freedom (Ferris 62, McCarty 33). But there's much more to know about Tubman. In fact, she is one of the ten most unforgettable black women (Norment 106). What makes her so unforgettable?

At about age thirty, Tubman escaped slavery. Only five feet tall (Chang 12), she soon became a military giant (Colman 62-63). By age forty, Tubman was already called "the General" (Bentley 95). The label stuck. Then, during the Civil War, she even "gained the respect of the Union officers" (Bentley 104). In fact, until the 1989 Panama Invasion, Tubman was the only woman - black or white - in American history to lead a military attack ("First Woman" 18). Why was she "General" Tubman?

Her military mind earned her the label. That military mind made her disciplined, creative, and bold - a hero.

Any paperback war hero must be disciplined. General Tubman was such a hero. Once as she led some runaway slaves to freedom, one man grew tired, cold, and hungry. He wanted to give up. Like a general in battle, Tubman pointed a pistol at his head and said, "Move or die" (Colman 63). Any slave who tried to run away but gave up would be beaten until he talked. Tubman "would allow no one to betray her routes and secrets" (Taylor 50). It took a tough woman to threaten to kill a fellow runaway.

In military style, she was even tough on her family. When Tubman planned to take her brothers to freedom, one brother was late. His wife was having a baby. Even though he begged Tubman to wait, military discipline would not let her. Months later, she returned home and showed the same discipline. It was Christmas Eve. She really wanted to see her parents, but she knew if their master questioned them, her parents could never lie. So Harriet's mother never knew her daughter was home. Harriet's father brought food, but he was blindfolded. That way, he could honestly say he never saw his children the whole day (McClard 88). Tubman's discipline helped her give up seeing her family on Christmas.

The tough, disciplined Harriet Tubman did what she did without worrying about what might happen to her. As one writer said, Harriet Tubman had "utter disregard of consequences" (Taylor 55). For instance, she never worried about being caught by slave hunters, even when the reward for her hit $40,000 (Ferris 57). Because she never worried about consequences, she also became a leader of the guerrilla fighters (Conrad 164). These were volunteers who sneaked into Rebel territory, raided the plantations, and set slaves free. During the Civil War, her guerrilla plans "created such a total effect . . . that the prolonged guerrilla operation can only be called the Battle of the Underground, and it must be compared to the victorious command of a major front in the Civil War itself" (Conrad 112). Yes, Tubman was one tough, disciplined woman!

In addition to being tough, General Tubman was also creative. For instance, to protect herself and

other runaways, Tubman carried forged passes that
fooled the patrols watching for runaway slaves. She
and other conductors also developed a military-like
code based on the Bible. One message she dictated
and sent home said, "Read my letter to the old folks,
and give my love to them, and tell my brothers to
be always watching unto prayer, and when the good
ship of Zion comes along, to be ready to step
aboard" (McClard 86). The coded letter meant her
brothers should always be ready (always prayerful)
to meet Tubman (their "savior") no matter when she
arrived. She could "save" them (take them to Zion)
if they were ready. The code kept her escape plan a
secret.

Her creativity also showed in her many
disguises. Once she sat "reading" a book while slave
catchers watched. Her heart pounded for fear she had
the book upside down (Colman 63)! The slave catchers
finally left. They said the Harriet Tubman they were
looking for couldn't read. Another time she dressed
as an old woman and tied live chickens to her belt.
When she saw her former master, she let the chickens
loose. Then she chased them, like an old woman. Her

creative disguise made the master laugh so hard he never recognized her (Chang 12).

Later, she worked as a spy during the Civil War. Her superiors thought she was "probably better qualified than any white spy to gather information" (Chang 55). They were right! She followed routes she knew from her Underground Railroad days. Along the way, she gained the trust of local blacks. They told her how and where explosives were hidden in the rivers. Tubman then led a successful raid up South Carolina's Combahee River. How? She knew exactly where to send the riverboat pilots around the explosives (Chang 55).

Military success never comes to the weak of heart. Tubman's boldness made her a hero early in life. During her Underground Railroad days, she was so bold that she hitched up a slave owner's horse and buggy, hid his escaping slaves in it, and drove away under his nose (Colman 63). The rescue of her own parents from slavery, though, was one of her boldest military plans. By tying them under a wagon, she rescued them from her own former owner! That earned

Neal 6

her the reputation of "accomplished artist and daring revolutionary" (Taylor 70).

Shortly after, the public saw Tubman's boldness at the Charles Nalle Trial. Even though he had escaped ten years earlier, Nalle was being returned to his master under the Fugitive Slave Act. The crowd outside the courthouse was cheering for Nalle, but Tubman did more than cheer. She planned his escape. When the judge made his decision, Tubman went into action. She fought with the policemen while Nalle ran out to a waiting wagon. She was "repeatedly beaten over the head with policemen's clubs, but she never for a moment released her hold . . . [and] suffered their blows without flinching" (Taylor 13-15). Then she escaped with Nalle. Her bold behavior made headlines in the next day's papers (Taylor 15).

Her boldness extended through the Civil War. According to General Rufus Saxton, Tubman "made many raids inside the enemy's lines, displaying remarkable courage, zeal, and fidelity" (Colman 70). The Union put Tubman in "charge of the Intelligence Service of the Department, [put] espionage . . . under her direction, and [made her] liaison between her colored aides and [three] generals" (Conrad 166). A Boston newspaper, <u>The Commonwealth</u>, reported that Tubman and her troops struck "terror into the heart of rebeldom, brought off near 800 slaves and thousands of dollars worth of property, without losing a man or receiving a scratch. It was a glorious consummation" (Colman 68) for the bold little woman.

Tubman was so much a military giant that the caption under her photograph calls her "the old fighter [with] her usual unflinching gaze" (Taylor 103). Sadly, however, the United States Congress never gave Tubman credit for her work. In fact, she received a government pension only because she was a widow of a Civil War veteran. "Prominent people tried to get Congress to pay Tubman for her Civil War service. But Congress refused" (Colman 83). Still, at her military funeral, "old soldiers stood at crisp attention, mourners bowed their heads, a bugler played taps, and the flag of the United States snapped in the breeze" (Taylor 104). Finally, in 1990, Congress set aside March 10, the date of her death, as Harriet Tubman Day (McCarty 33).

Neal 8

Works Cited

Bentley, Judith. <u>Harriet Tubman</u>. New York: Franklin
    Watts, 1990.

Chang, Ina. <u>A Separate Battle: Women and the Civil
    War</u>. New York: Lodestar Books, 1991.

Colman, Penny. <u>Spies! Women in the Civil War</u>.
    Cincinnati: Betterway Books, 1992.

Conrad, Earl. <u>Harriet Tubman</u>. New York: Paul S.
    Eriksson, Inc., 1969.

Ferris, Jeri. <u>Go Free or Die: A Story about Harriet
    Tubman</u>. Minneapolis: Carolrhoda Books, Inc.,
    1988.

"First Woman to Lead U.S. Troops Was Black, Not
    White." <u>Jet</u> 22 Jan. 1990: 18.

McCarty, Laura P. "Bound for Freedom." <u>National
    Parks</u>. Nov./Dec. 1991: 32-36. SIRS Researcher.
    "1992 History." 23.

McClard, Megan. <u>Harriet Tubman: Slavery and the
    Underground Railroad</u>. The History of the Civil
    War Series. New York: Silver Burdett Press,
    1991.

Norment, Lynn. "Ten Most Unforgettable Black Women."
    <u>Ebony</u> Feb. 1990: 104+.

Neal 9

Taylor, M. W. <u>Harriet Tubman: Antislavery Activist</u>.

Black Americans of Achievement Series. New

York: Chelsea House Publishers, 1991.

My Story: The Red-Tailed Hawk

by

Juan Sanchez

Science II

Mr. McKenney

21 January 19-

My Story: The Red-Tailed Hawk

In a patch of goldenrod blooming at the edge of the woods, I lay still. My dark brown and mottled gray feathers hid me among the weeds. My left wing throbbed near the joint. I could not fly.

Four days ago I had been on my usual perch. (See my portrait on page 3.) From a look-out (Pearson and others 71) on the tallest limb of a seventy-foot dead tree (Robbins and others 70), I was hunting for small rodents. My head cocked, I watched straight ahead to the corn field. I can always find mice there after the harvest. At the same time I watched to the side (Ripper 18). There, three men moved along the road. They slowed, and one of them pointed a stick-like thing at me. I flew, but as I did there was a loud crack. Something happened. My left wing hurt. I struggled and crashed into the weeds. I lay still, heart pounding, wing aching. The men laughed. I knew then for the first time in my eighteen months that humans, along with the stick-like thing, were my enemy (Ripper 63). Together, they killed.

Sanchez 3

Fortunately, however, I was alive - not well, but alive. For three days, without food, I lay near death. My body temperature dropped six degrees into what is called regulated hypothermia. It left me sleepy and slow but helped me survive (Ehrlich and others 153).

The third night a fox prowled nearby, sniffing, and caught my scent. In spite of my sluggishness, I went into full mantle. That's when I stick all my feathers straight out (Wallig 29) to make me look bigger and meaner than my six pounds (Wallig 146). I let out a high scream and then hissed (Robbins and others 70). The fox backed off. But my scent was too tempting. He crouched, inched forward, and I saw him ready to spring. Survival instincts gave me strength. As he pounced, I flopped over on my back. With beak and talons flying (Ripper 25), I sliced across his nose and face, ripping at his throat. He yelped and ran. My heart pounded. I was exhausted.

On the fourth day I sat dead still watching, hoping. A field mouse roamed nearby. Finally, it came close enough for me to snatch and hold in my talons. I tore the mouse into little pieces (Lanyon 43) and ate everything - fur, feet, and bones (Switzer 31). I began feeling stronger.

After so many days of neglect, I needed grooming. First I wiped my beak from side to side on a nearby branch. Then I cleaned every bit of the mouse remains from my feet until the black claws gleamed against my tannish-yellow feet (Wallig 22, 7). In August, I had molted and in about four weeks

Sanchez 5

dropped all my old, ragged feathers. Now I preened. I straightened each feather, pulled each through my bill, and cleaned it. Finally, from the uropygial gland at the base of my tail (Corral 27, 26), I spread oil on the clean feathers. While I would have liked a bath, that would have to wait until I could fly.

By the next day, my stomach had digested the mouse and sorted out the food from the garbage. I spit up the pellet of garbage (Switzer 31) and felt hungry again. If I were to survive, I had to hunt. The time had come to test my wings. I flew a few feet, wobbled, stopped to rest, and tried again. Each time I felt stronger. Each time the bad wing worked better. Each time I flew just a bit farther. I was glad the wound was only minor. After yet another day, I was almost airborne.

Finally, on the sixth day, I caught a thermal. It's like a swirling doughnut of warm air that rises as the sun warms the air near the ground (Switzer 14). I soared! My fifty-inch wing span (Ripper 14) and fan-like tail typical of us buteos once again put me a mile high. With eyes ten times stronger than humans', I watched for rodents on the ground (Switzer 11, 5). If humans only understood that they and we are not after the same game! My favorite food is limited almost entirely to rodents (Ripper 10).

The rest of the mild winter passed quietly. As a hunter, I help the balance of nature. By taking mostly the "unwary, sick, or unskilled members of prey" (Switzer 22), I help the healthiest survive.

In early spring, I began to notice another red-tail in my territory. You see, I may travel fifty to seventy-five miles a day (Ripper 41). Even though my territory covers more than a million square meters (Corral 156), rarely does another red-tail come around. This one, however, was beautiful. It was larger than I, so I was sure it was a female (Ehrlich and others 243). She looked dumpy and slow when roosting, but wow! was she ever sleek when diving (Ripper 15). One day I watched as she hunted. She "went into the magnificent stoop for which hawks are famous" (Wallig 114). Her wings and tail were almost closed. Her body was stretched out long and slim, her feet pressed back. Gorgeous!

Sanchez 7

As the days passed, the weather warmed. In another month leaves would be on the trees (Ripper 53). I began hunting closer to the female. Soon we began soaring together, and I showed off my best flying. I spiraled, crossed, and recrossed. She circled with me. Then I followed behind and above. It was a grand ballet in the air. Finally, we touched and locked feet in the air (Switzer 33). What a show! When she landed on a tall snag, I offered her a mouse (Ehrlich and others 232).

She chose the nesting site. One site I liked she refused. Her last year's nest there was torn apart by high winds (Wallig 138). Instead, she chose the crotch of a large tree, a safe spot about sixty feet high. Together we gathered sticks and twigs and built a big bulky nest. Big enough to hold our family-to-be, it still had room for us to land. Next we lined it with inner bark strips, evergreen sprigs, and green leaves (Ehrlich and others 232). Everything else done, my mate lined the nest with her breast feathers. The bare patch left on her breast has extra blood vessels. That gives added warmth to the eggs (Switzer 38).

There were three eggs, bluish white with light brown spots. We took turns sitting on the eggs, but she did more than her share. In about 35 days, the first chick hatched. The others followed every other day, just as the eggs were laid (Lanyon 127). We found ourselves proud parents of three nearly naked, down-covered babies. They were always hungry. Because young ones eat their weight in food every day, we worked hard every daylight minute to feed them and ourselves (Ehrlich and others 232). On rainy days, it was harder to find enough food. That's because one of us had to stay with the babies to keep them dry. Their down doesn't shed water like our feathers do.

Once some humans came up to our nesting tree. Remembering them as the enemy, I screeched and screamed and dove toward them with talons stuck out. They left us alone after that (Switzer 43, 41). Not all of us are so lucky. Sometimes humans steal young hawks.

In 45 days, our babies were ready to leave the nest (Ehrlich and others 232). Their flight feathers were in place (Ripper 55). How fast they had grown!

Their first flight was funny! They literally fell out of the nest and felt the air under their wings. Then they began taking short hops with us (Wallig 194). Their plumage was still dull and streaked. They did not yet have our rust-colored tail feathers (Bull and Farrand 638). But we were pleased with our little family. They soon learned to hunt. At first they hovered and dropped too fast on their targets (Ehrlich and others 225). Later they learned to soar and make soundless attacks (Ripper 17). Finally they learned to judge distances, a real trick when diving on moving prey (Switzer 18)!

The years have passed, one much like another. Now I'm three (Lanyon 149). Humans have invaded my territory in a big way. Their huge, noisy machines have cut a path that has no end. Then they put two wide strips of something hard along that path and left a wide grassy part down the middle and along each side. Without knowing, they have created a paradise for me! Mice, shrews, and voles are easy to see and catch in this new grassy place. In the late summer I sit in the sun for hours on fence posts along the path. I don't mind the sun because a strip of bone over each eye acts like a sun visor (Ripper 20). My three sets of eyelids protect me, too. I blink with my lower lid, which moves up to my upper lid. The third lid moves side to side. It clears and moistens my eyes. Sometimes I fall asleep sitting there, but I don't lose my balance. You see, the three toes in front and one in back act like a lock when I'm asleep (Switzer 21, 29). Only the crows harass me. They chase me when I fly and generally annoy me when I'm perched hunting. Otherwise, life is grand. What more could a red-tailed hawk want?

*   *   *   *   *

A month later, the red-tailed hawk dove for a shrew running along the highway median. At that instant, roaring along at 65 miles an hour, a tractor-trailer truck reached the spot where the hawk would have caught the shrew. The hawk fell, lifeless, from one of the more common causes of death (Despot). Wind from the speeding vehicles blasted the once perfect feathers. Within hours, crows pecked at his carcass, feeding on the carrion.

Sanchez 11

Works Cited

Bull, John, and John Farrand, Jr. <u>The Audubon
    Society Field Guide to North American Birds,
    Eastern Region</u>. New York: Alfred A. Knopf, 1977.

Corral, Michael. <u>The World of Birds: A Layman's
    Guide to Ornithology</u>. Chester, CT: The Globe
    Pequot Press, 1989.

Despot, Thomas. Sugar Ridge Fish and Wildlife
    biologist. Interview. November 30, 1994.

Ehrlich, Paul R., David S. Dobkin, and Darryl Wheye.
    <u>The Birder's Handbook: A Field Guide to the
    Natural History of North American Birds</u>. New
    York: Simon and Schuster, Inc., 1988.

Lanyon, Wesley E. <u>Biology of Birds</u>. Garden City,
    NY: The Natural History Press, 1963.

Pearson, T. Gilbert, and others, eds. <u>Birds of
    America</u>. Garden City, NY: Garden City Books,
    1917.

Ripper, Charles L. <u>Hawks</u>. New York: William Morrow
    & Company, 1956.

Robbins, Chandler S., Bertel Bruun, and Herbert S.
    Zim. <u>Birds of North America: A Guide to Field
    Identification</u>. New York: Golden Press, 1966.

Sanchez 12

Switzer, Merebeth. <u>Hawks</u>. Danbury, CT: Grober

Educational Corporation, 1986.

Wallig, Gaird.   <u>A Red-Tailed Hawk Named Bucket</u>.

Millbrae, CA: Celestial Arts, 1980.

My Story: The Red-Tailed Hawk
(Hypermedia Program)

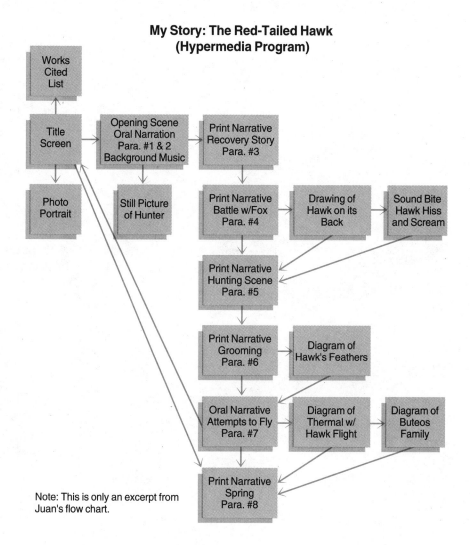

Note: This is only an excerpt from Juan's flow chart.

Trails to the Klondike

by

Jarrod Johnson

English I

Ms. Gant

24 January 19-

Table of Contents

Johnson 3

Dear Readers,

    Gold! It makes men do strange things. In 1898 gold rushers raced to the Klondike. These tough men faced below-zero weather and huge mountains in the Yukon Territory, but they struggled on.

    Three main trails led these men (and a few women) to the gold fields: the Ashcroft Trail from Vancouver, the White Pass Trail from Skagway, and the Chilkoot Trail from Dyea. The map on page 5 compares the routes (Berton, <u>Rush</u> 182, 275, 316).

    To tell about the problems they faced, three fictional men have written to you. Philip writes to you about the Ashcroft Trail; Jed, about the White Pass; and Milford about the Chilkoot. The Ashcroft Trail had few travelers. Fewer still reached the Klondike. On the other hand, the Chilkoot was the most popular. Travelers there were also most likely to succeed.

    Remember this as each man tells about the trail he followed: he carried about 2000 pounds - a ton! - of supplies. No matter which trail he followed, he crossed the mountains into the Yukon Territory. Each hauled his ton of supplies on his back. He did

Johnson 4

it in relay trips through mud, rain, floods, ice, snow, and blizzard winds.

Here are their letters. They help us understand what Robert Service meant when he wrote in his poem "The Prospector,"

It was my dream that made it good, my dream that
 made me go
To lands of dread and death disprized of man;
But oh, I've known a glory that their hearts
 will never know,
When I picked the first big nugget from my pan
 (Service 58).

I hope you enjoy the letters.

Sincerely,

Jarrod

Jarrod

Johnson 5

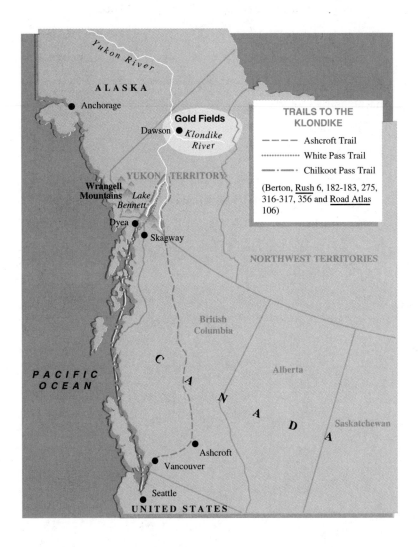

TRAILS TO THE
KLONDIKE

– – – – Ashcroft Trail

················ White Pass Trail

– · – · – Chilkoot Pass Trail

(Berton, <u>Rush</u> 6, 182-183, 275,
316-317, 356 and <u>Road Atlas</u>
106)

Johnson 6

Required Provisions

400 lbs. flour, 50 lbs. cornmeal
50 lbs. oatmeal, 35 lbs. rice
100 lbs. beans, 40 lbs. candles
100 lbs. sugar, 8 lbs. bake pwdr.
200 lbs. bacon, 2 lbs. soda
36 yeast cakes, 15 lbs. salt
1lb. pepper, 1/2 lb. mustard
1/4 lb. ginger, 24 lbs. coffee
75 lbs dried fruits, 5 lbs. tea
25 lbs. dried fish, 48 tins milk
50 lbs. dried onions
50 lbs. dried potatoes
5 bars laundry soap
60 boxes matches
25 cans butter
15 lbs. soup vegetables
5 yrds. mosquito netting

steel stove, gold pan, 9 buckets,
cup, plate, butcher knife, fork,
2 spoons, 2 fry pans, coffeepot,
pick, hand saw, whipsaw,
whetstone, hatchet, 2 shovels,
3 files, drawknife, axe, 3 chisels,
20 lbs. nails, hammer, compass,
square, sled, 200ft. rope,
15 lbs. pitch, 10 lbs. oakum, tent
3 suits underwear, mackinaw coat,
2 pr. mackinaw pants,
rubber-lined coat, 12 pr. socks,
6 pr. mittens, 2 overshirts,
2 pr. boots, 2 pr. shoes,
4 blankets, 4 towels, 2 pr. overalls,
suit of oil clothing

(Berton, Fever 253-254)

August 13, 1898

Dear Friends,

Well, so you want to know about a stampeder's problems on the Ashcroft Trail? I'm a good one to ask. I traveled that way. Took me over a year.

So let me tell you about it. I took the Ashcroft because it's the poor man's trail, the only way to get here without going by ship. Nothing wrong with ships, you understand. They just cost, like everything.

Now, I left Vancouver and traveled until the snows came. The deep stuff, I mean. Too deep to walk. Then several of us joined up and built a cabin. Come spring thaw, we set off again.

Turned out, the Ashcroft was much worse than we thought. In fact, it's called the Long Trail - all 1000 miles of it (Berton, Rush 274) to the Yukon River. Then it's another 1000 miles down the river to the gold fields. Easy floating, though.

Everybody back in Vancouver painted a pretty picture of this route. Said it followed the old telegraph route. Then right down the river to

Johnson 8

the Klondike. But they sort of ignored the gory details (Berton, <u>Fever</u> 224-225). It's a trail of death.

The trail was also worse for the rain. Rained almost every day. Always wet. Always mud. Everywhere. If you ask me, the trail is more like a "thousand-mile rut" (Berton, <u>Fever</u> 225). Oh, it was terrible the way horses sank belly-deep in that mud (Berton, <u>Rush</u> 275-276). Mosquitoes and black flies were so bad that sometimes it was hard to breathe. In fact, one time I saw bugs swarming a horse so bad that it finally died (McNeer 88). Worst of all, no grass grows along the trail - only poisonous weeds. Horses starved left and right. We lost all of ours. When the horses died, men "shouldered bulging packs and continued on foot" (McNeer 89). Some of the men died, too. It was bad.

Sometimes men went crazy from all the hardships. One man we met kept asking "Where's the gold?" We offered him food, but he kept asking for gold. Finally, when we reached the River and he found out he had another 1000 miles to go, he just blew out his brains.

Johnson 9

One day I saw a wallet nailed to a tree. Funny thing. So I looked. "Inside were money and a letter of farewell to a relative in Ohio" (Berton, <u>Fever</u> 229, 227). I left it. Someone will get it to Ohio. Nobody would steal from another stampeder. I can't help wondering, though, what happened to the man who owned it.

So it was a hard trip, but I'm okay. In fact, I'm working long days at a placer mine. Finding gold, too! Sometimes lots of it. When I come home, though, I'm coming by ship. I can pay now!

Respectfully yours,

Philip

Philip

August 2, 1898

Dear Friends,

    I can tell you all about the White Pass Trail. The trail starts out wide, smooth, and easy. Then the hills become mountains, and the mountains disappear in the clouds. The trail gets its name from the pass through the mountains.

    The pass was the worst part. Steep and crooked. On the very edge of sheer drops. We were all bent over from the weight of our packs. If you look down like that, you get real dizzy. I heard say not to look down. I didn't. A fellow behind me, well it was awful. He looked (McNeer 45). I didn't turn, just heard him scream. I had nightmares for weeks. Some say that "of the 5000 men who tried [the White Pass trail], . . . scarcely 500" (Berton, Stampede 84) made it.

    The real trouble was getting all my gear over the pass. Took twenty-one trips. Here's how it worked. I hauled as much as I could about six miles. Then I stacked that load beside the trail and went back for another. Since everybody was doing the same

thing, nobody bothered anybody else's stuff. To get
all my gear the 45 miles, I walked close to 900
miles.

Lately I've heard the White Pass called Dead
Horse Trail. Folks can't take horses up the
Chilkoot, so they take the parallel White Pass. Sad
to say, it's a death trap (Hunt 46). I heard that
3000 horses died along the trail. The real problem
is that lots of fellows never tended a horse before
and don't know head from tail. It'd make you sick to
see the way some animals were treated. "One man was
jabbing at his horse's flanks with a knife to make
him keep moving. The creature hobbled to the edge of
a precipice, looked down for a moment, and
deliberately jumped" (Poynter 64-5). There was also
a horse that had broken its leg

> where the trail squeezed between two huge
> boulders. The horse's pack had been removed,
> and someone had knocked it on the head with an
> ax; then traffic was resumed directly across the
> still warm body. . . . That evening there was
> not a vestige of the carcass left, save for the
> head on one side of the trail and the tail on

Johnson 12

the other. The beast had literally been ground
into the earth by the human machine. (Berton,
Fever 155)

A man up here named Jack London said it all: "Their
hearts turned to stone - those which did not break -
and they became beasts, the men on the Dead Horse
Trail" (Berton, Rush 187). I'll never forget what I
saw. I'm ashamed of the human race for what happened
on that 45 miles of switchback trail.

But I think things are better now. I hear
they've built a railroad through the White Pass.

Yours truly,

Jed

Jed

Johnson 13

August 10, 1898

Dear Friends,

    Summer on the Eldorado! Not like last winter's
seventy below! Working twenty hours a day now.
Never gets dark here in summer, you know.

    So you want to hear about the Chilkoot? Well,
it's 600 feet higher than White Pass. Ten miles
shorter. It's not easy, but 22,000 people have come
that way. More than by any other route (McNeer 53)!
Cross in winter; get to Lake Bennett by spring thaw.
Float the rest of the way. Here's the way it went
for me.

    I bought supplies in Seattle. You see, the
Canadian Mounties check everybody at the border. If
you don't have the necessities, they turn you back.
So I stocked up in Seattle. Best prices there, you
know.

    From there I shipped out to Dyea. No dock
there. Shallow water way out. So the shippers threw
all our stuff on the beach. Had to run around like
crazy to find everything before the tide washed it
out (Berton, Rush 313).

Johnson 14

From Dyea, it took me three months to get over the pass (McNeer 57). We moved stuff in stages up the mountains. Finally, at Sheep Camp, we started through the pass. A 45 degree climb, "so steep that a man has to bend only slightly to touch the snow ahead of him" (McNeer 57). Took about six hours to make the four miles to the top with a 50-pound pack (McNeer 57). Sometimes somebody would fall. You know - steep climb, high altitude, heavy pack. Well, when that happened, we just walked around him. Didn't even speak. When I think now, it's embarrassing. Then it was everyone for himself. Why, if you just stepped out of line to rest, it would take hours to get in the line again (Berton, Stampede 100).

At the top of the pass, I unloaded my gear. Then slid lickety-split on my rear down a snow chute (Berton, Stampede 101), reloaded, and started over. Over and over again and again. Trip after trip. So many times I lost count. When I think about that climb, I shake my head at what some people hauled over. The strangest was "a couple. . . [who] made trips up and down over Chilkoot Pass all winter and

Johnson 15

spring. Piece by piece they brought over a small steamboat" (McNeer 59)!

After the pass, it was all down hill. Then a long float down the Yukon. And then the gold fields. And here I am.

Best wishes, folks. When I come home, I'll ride the new tramway down to Sheep Camp (Greever 349) and pay to have my gold hauled out. I won't carry anything myself. Not this time!

Yours,

Milford

Milford

Studying Three Model Reports

Number of Gold Rushers Attempting and Succeeding to Reach the Klondike on the Three Major Trails

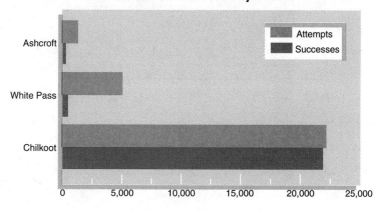

Sources: McNeer 53; Burton, Fever 224; Burton, Stampede 84

Johnson 17

Works Cited

Berton, Pierre. <u>Klondike: The Last Great Gold Rush</u>
     <u>1896-1899</u>. Rev. ed.   Toronto: Penguin Books,
     1972.

---. <u>The Klondike Fever: The Life and Death of</u>
     <u>the Last Great Gold Rush</u>. New York: Knopf,
     1958.

---. <u>Stampede for Gold: The Story of the Klondike</u>.
     New York: Knopf, 1955.

Greever, William S. <u>The Bonanza West: The Story</u>
     <u>of the Western Mining Rushes, 1848-1900</u>.
     Norman, OK: University of Oklahoma Press,
     1963.

Hunt, William R. <u>North of 530: the Wild Days of the</u>
     <u>Alaska-Yukon Mining Frontier, 1870-1914</u>. New
     York: Macmillan, 1974.

"Klondike." <u>Encyclopedia Americana</u>. 1993.

McNeer, May Younge. <u>The Alaska Gold Rush</u>. New York:
     Random House, 1960.

Poynter, Margaret. <u>Gold Rush: The Yukon Stampede of</u>
     <u>1898</u>. New York: Atheneum, 1979.

<u>Road Atlas</u>. "Canada." Chicago: Rand McNally, 1992.

Service, Robert. <u>The Best of Robert Service</u>.

    Toronto: McGraw-Hill Ryerson, 1953.

<u>Yukon Passage</u>. Vidoerecording. Washington, D.C.:

    The National Geographic Society, 1977.

Index

A

Attention, catching reader's, 169–172
Audience, 26, 28–30, 40–41, 43–44

B

Body, 173–185, 192
Brackets, 127–128
Bibliography cards, 89–109
  for books, 95–96, 102–103
  for electronic media, 101–102, 104
  for encyclopedia articles, 100
  for magazines, 97–99, 103
  for newspapers, 97–98, 103
  for other print and nonprint resources, 103–104

C

Catalog, card, 65–71, 79, 86–87
  computer, 71–74, 79, 81
CD-ROM, 22, 74, 81, 101–102
Checklist, 16, 42, 55–56, 84, 106–107, 138,160, 190–191, 208, 238–239
Codes, 118, 179–181, 190, 213–218
Common knowledge, defined, 184
Concluding sentence, 183
Conclusion, 185–187, 192
Connecting words, 177, 182–183, 199–202, 209–210
Computer hint, 7, 13, 22, 31, 33, 34, 64, 71, 73, 74, 90, 101, 113, 119, 144, 156, 166, 167, 178, 199, 202, 204, 222, 223, 224, 228, 231, 232
Critical thinking hint, 9, 25, 37, 38, 48, 49, 67, 69, 77, 92, 98,

Index